D0105724

Pastor Choco leads by example. Ir[...] powerful personal testimonies of how living in the fullness of Christ has changed his life, changed his church and the life of those around him. This book helps others to experience this same rich, abundant life.

Roma Downey, actor and producer,
president of LightWorkers Media

Pastor Choco has a heart for the lost, for those who are hurting, and for the downtrodden. *Move into More* reminds us that serving others should be a priority of all Christ followers. We receive blessings from God when we pour blessings into the lives of others.

Kirk Cameron, actor and producer

Move into More is for anyone who wants insight on God's blessings. Using biblical principles and examples, Pastor Choco helps readers understand the importance of not only receiving but freely sharing God's blessings.

Ed Stetzer, Billy Graham Distinguished
Chair, Wheaton College

JUN - - 2018

MOVE into MORE

Mar-11-2018

5991201801_WB_C_16

MOVE into MORE

The Limitless Surprises
of a Faithful God

Choco De Jesús

ZONDERVAN

Move into More
Copyright © 2018 by Wilfredo De Jesús

Requests for information should be addressed to:
Zondervan, *3900 Sparks Dr. SE, Grand Rapids, Michigan 49546*

ISBN 978-0-310-35314-0 (audio)

ISBN 978-0-310-34954-9 (ebook)

Library of Congress Cataloging-in-Publication Data

Names: De Jesus, Wilfredo, author.
Title: Move into more: the limitless surprises of a faithful God / Choco De Jesus.
Description: Grand Rapids, Michigan : Zondervan, [2018]
Identifiers: LCCN 2017047726 | ISBN 9780310349921 (softcover)
Subjects: LCSH: Christian life.
Classification: LCC BV4501.3 .D3985 2018 | DDC 248.4—dc23 LC record available at
    https://lccn.loc.gov/2017047726

All Scripture quotations, unless otherwise indicated, are taken from The Holy Bible,
New International Version®, NIV®. Copyright © 1973, 1978, 1984, 2011 by Biblica,
Inc.® Used by permission of Zondervan. All rights reserved worldwide. www.
Zondervan.com. The "NIV" and "New International Version" are trademarks registered
in the United States Patent and Trademark Office by Biblica, Inc.®

Scripture quotations marked ESV are taken from the ESV® Bible (The Holy Bible,
English Standard Version®). Copyright © 2001 by Crossway, a publishing ministry of
Good News Publishers. Used by permission. All rights reserved.

Scripture quotations marked NKJV are taken the New King James Version®. © 1982 by
Thomas Nelson. Used by permission. All rights reserved.

Scripture quotations marked NLT are taken from the Holy Bible, New Living
Translation, © 1996, 2004, 2007, 2013, 2015 by Tyndale House Foundation. Used by
permission of Tyndale House Publishers, Inc., Carol Stream, Illinois 60188. All rights
reserved.

Any Internet addresses (websites, blogs, etc.) and telephone numbers in this book are
offered as a resource. They are not intended in any way to be or imply an endorsement by
Zondervan, nor does Zondervan vouch for the content of these sites and numbers for the
life of this book.

All rights reserved. No part of this publication may be reproduced, stored in a retrieval
system, or transmitted in any form or by any means—electronic, mechanical, photocopy,
recording, or any other—except for brief quotations in printed reviews, without the prior
permission of the publisher.

Published in association with The Quadrivium Group, Orlando Florida.

Cover photography: Iris Figueroa
Interior design: Kait Lamphere

First printing February 2018 / Printed in the United States of America

CONTENTS

FOREWORD

Never enough.

That's the message I hear from people, Christians and nonbelievers alike, more and more. Not enough time. Not enough money. Not enough energy to get everything done. Not enough joy. Not enough peace. Not enough hope to believe they will ever experience what they long for most.

Despite having more possessions and technological advances than any culture in history, we have fallen into a "scarcity mindset," the term psychologists use for people who have endured extreme deprivation and consequently assume enough is never enough. Usually this term applied to individuals growing up in extreme poverty, survivors of war, or others facing catastrophic conditions that made basic survival an everyday struggle. Only now, having a scarcity mindset has become an emotional default setting.

But that's the opposite experience of what the Christian life is supposed to be about. Jesus said, "I have come that they may have life, and have it to the full" (John 10:10). Repeatedly in the Bible we see the same message: God "is able to do immeasurably more than all we ask or imagine, according to his power that is at work within us" (Eph. 3:20). We're told, "Ask and it will be given to you; seek and you will find; knock and the door will be opened to you" (Matt. 7:7).

So obviously there's a problem, a disconnect somewhere. Because God has promised his followers a sense of fullness and abundance, a satisfaction and contentment, the "more to life" that you've always known has to be part of why you're here on this earth. Yet so many of us are not experiencing it.

Which is why I'm so glad my friend and fellow pastor Choco De Jesús has addressed this problem in a powerful, comprehensive, and truly inspiring study of what it means to live in the fullness God promises us. I don't know anyone better qualified than Pastor Choco to guide us in an exploration of what it means to move into more. He's one of the most joyful, peaceful, and intensely passionate followers of Jesus I know. He clearly lives in that fullness, that abundant life, Jesus said He came to bring.

Choco knows what more is all about. It's not about possessions or constant happiness or the size of your bank account. Pure and simple, it's about knowing God and relying on him as your source for everything. It's about drawing closer to him and moving into more—more to enjoy, more to share, more to invest for what matters most.

So if you're exhausted by never having enough, if you're running on fumes and wondering why life feels so hard, then this book is for you. Get ready to encounter the living God and the power, purpose, and provision of the Holy Spirit. Get ready to move into more!

MARK BATTERSON

MORE THAN
MEETS THE EYE

*"No eye has seen, no ear has heard, and no mind
has imagined what God has prepared for those who
love him."*

—1 CORINTHIANS 2:9 NLT

L ess is the new more.

Sounds *loco*, I know, but let me explain. I keep running across speakers, books, blogs, and conferences focused on helping people have less—less stuff cluttering up their homes, fewer activities and responsibilities filling up their schedules, and limited distractions from media, online sources, and social networks. We've become so overwhelmed by "having it all" that now we need help "losing it all" as we excavate and find ourselves again. As writer Kyle Chayka observed in a recent *New York Times Magazine* article: "People who have it all now seem to prefer having nothing at all."[1] This is the consequence of too much self-indulgence, consumer consumption, and a "never enough" attitude toward material possessions.

The irony to me—someone who grew up as a poor Puerto Rican kid in one of Chicago's toughest hoods—is the motivation behind these "less is more" pursuits: it's the same internal desire all of us have for something more in our lives. So wanting less really is about longing for more! Our culture has once again awakened to the fact that accumulating material stuff isn't the answer. We're not only realizing how too much clogs up our lives; we're also recognizing an absence of joy, peace, and satisfaction.

We're trying to get in touch with a spiritual longing, an emptiness inside us that only God can fill. There's nothing wrong—and a lot that's right—with getting rid of things we don't need in our lives. But we also have to clarify this yearning for more burning inside us. Having more stuff won't fill it. Having less stuff won't fill it.

Only God can give us the more we long for.

Never Enough

When I was growing up, there was never enough.

Not enough food in the house, not enough time for school and work, not enough money in my mother's purse. My mother used humor to hide our lack of money. I would ask for money, and she would respond with, "Oh yes, let me get you some from our money tree in the back." Or I would ask, "Why do we have to be on welfare?" and she would respond, "Because our money tree is not fully grown yet." We laughed, and it helped us to forget our worries.

Growing up in Humboldt Park, a notoriously tough Chicago neighborhood, I learned quickly not to want much, expect much, hope for much. That was just the way life was. My dad had abandoned our family, leaving my mom to raise six kids. She was doing the best she could, but we were like so many other Puerto Rican families there at the time: short on resources and long on problems. Problems like gangs, drugs, and police brutality. Problems that kept cycling through each new generation.

I watched my brothers get consumed by gangs and wondered why they couldn't see what they were doing. I witnessed friends, neighbors, and extended family members battle addiction, domestic abuse, and gang violence. I stood outside a corner grocery store when I was twelve years old, paralyzed by the angry mob rioting and looting businesses along the streets around me. Through it all, I kept thinking there had to be something better. There had to be more.

By age fourteen, I knew I'd found it. I signed up for a summer works program and was assigned to a community hub, which happened to be a church. My family practiced a cultural Catholicism, so I had some awareness of God, Jesus, and the Bible. But the people—especially the other kids like me—I met at this church were unlike anyone I'd met in my short life.

They were from the same battered neighborhoods and single-parent homes as mine, but they had something else going on. There was a sincerity, an authentic joy, a calm manner totally alien to me. They lacked the anger, mistrust, and skepticism that had become epidemic, and I couldn't understand it. When a group of other young teens asked if they could pray with me and then encircled me, I was ready to fight!

But they weren't there to hurt me—they were simply sharing the love of Jesus, which seemed to be the source of the "more" in their lives. I knew I wanted what they had, so I prayed and surrendered my heart to God. Immediately I sensed God's Spirit in a way that can only be described as supernatural and truly life-changing. Not long after this encounter with Christ, I accompanied my new Christian brothers and sisters to a conference, an event they promised would add fuel to the fire of my faith. The conference featured amazing preachers, Bible teachers, and speakers. After the main service, I was in tears, moved by God's Spirit within me, and I felt compelled to walk to the altar where others would pray for me.

As I knelt on those carpeted steps, a fourteen-year-old kid becoming a man, something incredible happened. An older lady came directly toward me, smiling. She put her hands on my shoulder and began praying. She told me that God had anointed me for amazing things, to advance his kingdom. She said, "God has a message for you: 'I have called you to be a great leader. Stay in my path. I will bless those who bless you, and I will curse those who curse you.'" At the time, I honestly had no idea what she was talking about but appreciated her kindness toward me.

About twenty minutes later, as I was making my way out of the hotel where the conference was being held, something really *extraño*—extraordinary, bizarre—happened. I had just gotten on the elevator when a nicely dressed businessman popped through the doors just as they were closing. He smiled at me. While I wasn't afraid of him, something about him made the hair on the back of my neck stand up.

"Have you not heard?" he said, still smiling. "I've called you to be a great leader. Stay in my path. I will bless those who bless you, and I will curse those who curse you."

Wow, I thought, *he must be related to the lady who prayed over me. Maybe this guy is her husband.*

Who knew an elevator ride could last so long? The gist of the message was almost identical to what the lady had prayed less than an hour before.

When the elevator stopped—*ding!*—I mumbled a quick "thank you" and dashed away before he really started to creep me out. I couldn't put my finger on it at the time, but something had just happened in that elevator, something supernatural that would affect me for the rest of my life.

Discovering More

I have thought of that crossroad moment many times in the thirty years since it happened. Not only does it remind me of God's love and power in my life, but when certain things take place, I think, *Aha! This must be what that prophetic word was about all those years ago.* As a volunteer youth leader for the same church where I invited Jesus into my life, I thought I'd discovered God's more. Then when I was promoted to regional youth leader for our denomination, I realized I must have been wrong—this was the more.

Then a few years later, I recalled the man on the elevator when I became a pastor. Surely, pastoring a church in Humboldt Park, the gang-infested neighborhood where I grew up, was the "more" of which I had been foretold. But then our church began to grow, with new ministries springing up along the way, then with new campuses erupting in other parts of the greater Chicago area. Then the Lord truly did a miracle and provided property for us to build our main campus church right smack in the middle of Humboldt Park. Next thing I know, I'm featured on the cover of *TIME Magazine*—me, Choco from the hood. Surely that was it, right?

Every time I encountered a new position of influence or season of elevation, I always assumed that *this* was the promise at last. But as I leaned into what God gave me and followed his guidance, I always found myself taking another leap of faith, another giant stride toward something I would never have dreamed, let alone attempted, on my own.

Going through door after door, step by step, I've discovered that God *always* has more. We not only never arrive where we think we will—we never reach the summit in this lifetime. We may feel stuck in a plateau, but it's not because God doesn't have more for us. There's always more! Jesus told us, "I came that they may have life and have it abundantly" (John 10:10 ESV). This full, rich, satisfying life is not about wealth and material possessions. It's not about fame and celebrity or political power. God's more is far better! It's infinite—there's no ceiling on what God can do when you let him.

Maybe you're thinking, *That's fine for you, Pastor Choco. I'm glad you had such a powerful, dramatic experience revealing God's more for your life. But I've never had anything like that happen to me. I want more from God, from my life, but I'm not sure how to experience it.*

My friend, God's more is not limited to me or to pastors or Puerto Ricans from Chicago! The abundant more Jesus came to bring is for all of us. As the angels told the shepherds at the birth of Christ, "Fear not, for behold, I bring you good news of great joy that will be for *all* the people. For unto you is born . . . a Savior, who is Christ the Lord" (Luke 2:10–11 ESV, emphasis added). God so loved the world (John 3:16), not just a few here and there, that he sacrificed his beloved only Son. This is the essence of the gospel, the good news that Jesus saves us from sin and death and instead gives us grace and life.

Don't settle for less than God's best for your life. He has something more waiting for you. God has promised and planned a richer, more fulfilling life than the one you're living right now. If you are willing to follow him faithfully, obey him lovingly, and yield to him consistently, you will be amazed. You may not have an "elevator experience" like I did, but God will reveal—and continue to reveal—what he has laid out for you. No matter where you are on your journey of faith, God wants to take you higher, stretch you farther, and hold you closer. His more has no boundaries and no limits. His Word promises you—and me, and everyone—that we can learn to live in his fullness.

Are you ready for more?

Then turn the page.

Chapter 1

MARKED BY GOD
FOR MORE

God loves each of us as if there were only one of us.
—AUGUSTINE

No one is more surprised than me to see where I am right now.

I remember my mother sending me to the corner store when I was a kid, probably around eleven or twelve years old. While I was willing to go and wanted to help out, I absolutely hated going. We had little money, so she often gave me food stamps to use for the items on her list. Stuffed deep in my pocket, those little coupons made me feel so ashamed. I felt like I carried a dark secret. I wasn't ashamed to be poor—that was just the way life was, for us and so many others. I was ashamed because using those food stamps felt like giving up, relying on the government, resigning myself to being a victim of circumstances.

So whenever my mother sent me shopping with those pink, green, and blue slips that reminded me of Monopoly money,

I acted like a spy on a secret mission. We lived in Humboldt Park, on the northwest side of Chicago, and while I wouldn't want to be on certain streets after dark, going to the store in broad daylight was relatively safe. I'd casually walk the couple of blocks from our apartment, but as soon as I turned the corner and spotted the store, I'd duck into the nearby alley. I'd watch the entrance of Sam's store to see how many people were coming and going, and more importantly, if I recognized any of them. Once the coast was clear, I'd make a run for it, dashing through the door as the bell above it rang.

"*Hola, Chocolate,*" Sam would say, looking up from ringing up a customer's purchase. The place smelled of tobacco and overripe fruit; it had high shelves and no windows except the ones by the door. I'd return his greeting and head down the produce aisle to scope out the place. Over the bins of potatoes and onions, I'd scan the faces of shoppers for anyone who might know me. If I saw kids I knew from school or the neighborhood, I'd rush to the candy aisle, buy a two-cent piece of bubble gum, and leave, before starting my surveillance all over again. If it wasn't too busy and I didn't know anyone, then I'd begin finding the items on *Mami*'s list.

Then, finally, the moment I dreaded the most: bringing out those crumpled coupons to pay for the food. If possible, I would wait until no one else was in line—not always easy on a Saturday afternoon—and then rush through the transaction as quickly as possible, worried a friend or neighbor might come in and see me with food stamps in hand. Sam could tell I was embarrassed and always spoke kindly to me, a certain familiar sadness in his eyes.

Even before I became a Christian and God set my life on a completely unexpected path, I knew I wasn't willing to settle for the kind of life I had been born into. I tried not to judge others, but the prospect of dropping out of school, living on food stamps, and juggling dead-end jobs made me determined to get out.

Even as a kid, I knew I wanted more.

Status Check

A few years ago, I was feeling a little out of my element, and a renowned educator and speaker was kind enough to help me prepare for an important speaking engagement. As I shared my story with him, this professional was surprised to hear how my life had unfolded and catapulted me into full-time ministry. He told me I was a "status inconsistency." That's the term sociologists use for someone whose "ascribed status"—in my case, a Puerto Rican male born into a large, single-parent family in inner-city Chicago—doesn't match their "achieved status"—a pastor of a thriving church, a husband for more than twenty-five years, a father of three and grandfather of one, a speaker and educator, a graduate student currently completing a doctorate.

I hadn't ended up as a high school dropout, gang member, day laborer, or felon, which, unfortunately, is how many with my ascribed status wind up. Based on statistics, I should not have escaped the socioeconomic and cultural barriers inhibiting so many people born into similar situations. But by the grace of God, I never followed the stereotypical script for my demographic. I became more than any sociologist ever could have predicted.

I became more than I ever dreamed because I discovered the exhilarating, limitless, unpredictable, overflowing life of God's more. And I'm not the only one with privileged access to his abundance. Once we accept Jesus into our hearts, we all become status inconsistencies.

We're no longer who we once were, no longer on the trajectory for a life like others with similar situations and characteristics. Paul described this dramatic change in a letter to the church at Corinth, listing those who will not inherit the kingdom of God—including idolaters, adulterers, liars, swindlers, and the sexually immoral—before revealing "that is what some of you were. But you were washed, you were sanctified, you were justified in the name of the Lord Jesus Christ and by the Spirit of our God" (1 Cor. 6:11). No matter how we grew up, what we've done or haven't done, or who we've been or haven't been, God meets us where we are. But he loves us too much to leave us there. Once we invite him into our lives, we're no longer living a life by default, feeling like a victim of circumstances. We become his new creation with the adventure of our lives ahead of us.

No matter how we grew up, what we've done or haven't done, or who we've been or haven't been, God meets us where we are.

We begin becoming all of who God created us to be.

Hearing and Believing

How do you know where you are in pursuit of more? In the Bible we're told, "And you also were included in Christ when you heard the message of truth, the gospel of your salvation. When you believed, you were marked in him with a seal, the promised Holy Spirit, who is a deposit guaranteeing our inheritance until the redemption of those who are God's possession—to the praise of his glory" (Eph. 1:13–14).

This passage lays out the four progressive steps to growing in faith, maturing as a follower of Jesus, and experiencing all that God has for you. It begins when you hear the "message of truth, the gospel of your salvation." For many people, like myself, this may have happened at a young age. You may have been blessed to grow up in a Christian home and accepted Jesus as your Savior while growing up. Others may have heard the good news of the gospel many times with their ears before they really heard it in their hearts. We must encounter God's truth inside our hearts if we want to begin our journey toward more.

After the message of salvation is heard, we must believe. To establish our relationship with God, we must believe by faith that Jesus is the Son of God. We must trust in the gift of salvation purchased by Christ's sacrifice on the cross. As I talk with many people who ask me why they're not experiencing God's more in their lives, it becomes clear they're not sure what they believe.

"I'm just not sure, Choco," they tell me. "I want to believe in the Bible and put my faith in Christ, but I wasn't around back then. If I haven't seen something firsthand, I don't know if I can believe in it."

There are many historical and theological ways to provide evidence for the truth of God's Word and the life, death, and resurrection of Jesus, but I usually take a simple approach. "Well," I say to these skeptics, "do you believe that George

Washington fought the British and went on to become our country's first president? Do you believe that our nation split in two and fought itself for several long, brutal years in the 1860s?"

"Sure," they say, "that's historical and can be proven."

"But were you there?" I ask them. "Why are you willing to believe what history books and school teachers say about George Washington or Abraham Lincoln but refuse to believe the Bible and the truth of what it says about Jesus Christ?"

These people may even want to believe. Until they make that leap of surrender and give themselves, including all their imperfect parts and broken pieces, to God by trusting in Jesus Christ, their spiritual growth can't take root. They remind me of the parable of the sower that Jesus told, specifically the seed that fell on rocky places. "It sprang up quickly, because the soil was shallow. But when the sun came up, the plants were scorched, and they withered because they had no root" (Matt. 13:5–6). Your faith must run deep throughout the soil of your life if you want to cultivate a belief that will not wither.

Lost and Found

Once you've heard and believed, then you're "marked in him with a seal, the promised Holy Spirit." When you open your heart to Christ and commit to following God, the gift of his Spirit comes to dwell in you as a comforter, guide, and holy presence. This is the reason Jesus left the earth after he had risen from the dead. He explained, "It is to your advantage that I go away, for if I do not go away, the Helper will not come to you. But if I go, I will send him to you. And when he comes, he will convict the world concerning sin and righteousness and judgment" (John 16:7–8 ESV).

While it was great to have Jesus walk this earth in the flesh, it's even better to have the Holy Spirit with us now. It's for our own good. Just imagine if Jesus were still here with us, walking around and ministering to people. Just imagine that you hear that he is preaching and teaching in some far-off country, so you, along with millions of others, book your ticket to travel to where he is, because everyone wants to be near Jesus. No matter where he would be, the news would spread, and millions of people would surround him at all times. We would not have the direct access to him like we do through the Holy Spirit. It's better now, because he lives and dwells in our hearts. We can have an intimate relationship with Jesus, which would be nearly impossible if he lived here with us in the flesh.

Jesus didn't come to live among us as a man throughout time and history; he came to die for our sins and leave us with the gift of the Spirit. Christ said, "I will ask the Father, and he will give you another Helper, to be with you forever, even the Spirit of truth, whom the world cannot receive, because it neither sees him nor knows him. You know him, for he dwells with you and will be in you" (John 14:16–17 ESV).

Paul phrased our reception of the Holy Spirit as being "marked in him with a seal." Seals were used in four different ways in Paul's day. First, a seal on a letter or document was a sign of authenticity. Leaders, officials, and royalty often sealed their letters with warm wax into which they pressed their unique insignia, crest, or title. The seal served as a sign of authenticity so no one else would mistake the letter as coming from anyone else.

We do the same thing with many of our own possessions, especially those of our kids. We sew name labels inside their clothes or use permanent marker to inscribe lunchboxes, sports equipment, and backpacks. With his Spirit sealing your relationship, God has marked you to show that he owns you. You are his child, and he is your Father. Sealed by God's ownership, you belong to him and will return to him.

Think of the way you check a suitcase before you get on a flight. The airline attendant has placed a tag on your bag identifying you as the owner, along with the bag's final destination. This ID label ensures that this bag belongs to you and will be waiting for you at your destination—well, most of the time.

I remember when my wife, Elizabeth, and I traveled to Australia. Unfortunately, our luggage didn't make it. Much to my wife's delight, we were forced to buy new clothes, which the airline paid for—much to my delight. A few days later, I answered a knock on our door and discovered a deliveryman with our suitcases. They had been halfway around the world, but they eventually made it back to us because of the scan tag that identified us as the owners.

Sometimes we drift away from God. Our drifting may be unintentional, the result of hectic schedules and overwhelming responsibilities. Or it may be a deliberate choice to go our own direction instead of God's. We end up like Adam and Eve in the garden, disobeying God and doing what we please instead of what he has told us to do.

Consider the way God told Jonah to go to the city of Nineveh and deliver God's message to the people there. Because he knew they wouldn't like what God had to say, Jonah rerouted his course and sailed for Tarshish. He didn't get far because a certain big fish reminded Jonah of who he belonged to and where he was supposed to go.

Seals also indicate the owner's approval. Think about the closing process when you buy a home or piece of property. Usually a title company certifies that the property's title is clear and transferred to your ownership. Their seal indicates that they guarantee the transaction as final and binding. No one else can challenge the purchase because the official title officer has sealed the deal.

Finally, seals are used as a warning or a sign of protection. When Jesus's body was brought down from the cross, Pilate told the Roman soldiers to place the royal seal on the stone used to seal Christ's tomb. Pilate feared that Jesus's followers might steal their master's body and claim that Jesus had risen, so he tried to warn off any would-be grave robbers that they were committing a crime against the Roman government. However, nothing could prevent Jesus from rising from the dead and leaving that tomb. Despite its intention, Pilate's seal failed.

God's seal on us through the Holy Spirit can never be breached or broken. God has promised to guard us and to help us overcome the temptations of our enemy, the devil. In God's Word we're told, "You, dear children, are from God and have overcome them, because the one who is in you is greater than the one who is in the world" (1 John 4:4). Just as we can't see the wind, we still acknowledge its force when we see it blow down trees, send paper flying, or mess up our hair. The power of the Holy Spirit is an invisible force that protects us. We aren't able to measure it, analyze it, or contain it, but the power of God's Spirit in our lives is undeniable.

Yes to More

Once you've been marked by God with the seal of his Holy Spirit, you mature in your faith and spiritually move from drinking milk to eating solid food. The old sinful habits and struggles lose their power as you spend time in God's Word and get to know him through prayer and time alone with him. Once the promise of salvation is yours and the Holy Spirit dwells in you, you begin growing, changing, and being transformed. The evidence of your spiritual growth and maturity is on display in how you think, talk, and act.

Our faithful obedience to God's Word and to the leading and prompting of the Holy Spirit conditions us for more. As we grow stronger, we begin swimming in the infinite ocean of God's more. We make our way upstream only to discover a larger lake ahead of us. Our obedience in small things conditions us and prepares us for more. God uses our obedience in our present situation to empower and equip us for the more he has for us ahead. If we're not willing to say yes and trust God with the more he has given us today, we won't be ready to be champions against the challenges of tomorrow.

If there's a secret to experiencing God's more, it's our willingness to say yes to God. That's the only reason my life has continued to exceed my wildest dreams. It's not that I don't work hard, because I do. And I know that God has given me certain gifts, just as he has done with you. But there's no way I can take credit for the amazing life, family, ministry, and platform with which God has blessed me and continues to bless me.

I've simply said yes every step of the way.

When I was fourteen and the woman spoke God's message

to me followed by the Anglo dude on the elevator, I was blown away. It was no coincidence that both of them spoke the exact same words to me, which I soon discovered was the promise God gave to Abraham: "I will make your name great, and you will be a blessing. I will bless those who bless you, and whoever curses you I will curse; and all peoples on earth will be blessed through you" (Gen. 12:2–3).

As a new believer, I wasn't able to fathom all that this word of God over me actually meant.

> *If there's a secret to experiencing God's more, it's our willingness to say yes to God.*

But I did know that I was marked by God and sealed by his Spirit. And I knew God always follows through and keeps his promises, which meant I couldn't waste time being a knuck-lehead and getting into trouble. After that experience, I knew God had more for me even though I wasn't sure what it would be. So in the meantime, I remained active in my church, kept serving our community through the city works program, and applied myself as best I could to my schoolwork. I took the verse that says, "Whatever your hand finds to do, do it with all your might" (Eccl. 9:10), to heart all because I knew God was up to something.

A few years later, I thought I had finally figured out what God had for me. I had been active in Royal Rangers, our fellowship's youth program for boys, throughout my time at our church. This organization is similar to the Boy Scouts but focuses on knowing God's Word and living out your faith. Because of my faithful participation, I got promoted to leadership and was asked to be the sectional chaplain for Royal Rangers for the state of Illinois.

The coolest part was that I got a special jacket with two stars on it, sort of like a general's uniform. I remember sitting at our Royal Rangers yearly banquet wearing that two-starred jacket. I had brought my pastor's daughter, Elizabeth, as my date and shared with her how God had prepared me for my new role. She agreed that surely this was the leadership role for which God had been preparing me!

Discovering More

A couple years later, however, I experienced another leap of leadership. Not long after Elizabeth and I were married, my new father-in-law asked me to drive him to the convention for our Midwest Latin District, comprised of eleven Midwestern states. In addition to being in the family, I also served on his pastoral team in a role we call an "armor-bearer." Right before we arrived, he said, "Oh, by the way, they're voting on a new youth president today; you should put your name on the ballot."

"Say *what?*" I asked.

"I sense God wants to increase your leadership responsibilities in the church, so I thought this might be the next step he has for you."

I couldn't disagree with both my pastor and my father-in-law, let alone God, so I put my name on the ballot and waited to see what would happen in the convention once the voting started. Ministers and pastoral staff from all eleven states were there, hundreds of the best and brightest leaders in our denominational district. When it came time for the candidates to introduce themselves, the first guy stood up, introduced himself, and said he had just completed his bachelor's degree at a nearby university. *Wow*, I thought, *there's no way I can compete with that dude.* The next candidate got up, introduced himself, and described his credentials. Then it was my turn. I stood up and said, "My name is Choco, and I'm a Sunday school teacher at my church." I couldn't think of anything else to say. But apparently I didn't need to.

I won by unanimous decision.

I couldn't believe it! There was no good reason why I won the vote unanimously except for God. The fact that I was chosen to be youth president for our district only made sense because I thought, *Oh, so this is what God has been preparing me for all along.*

I soon learned the role wasn't very glamorous. It was hard work and a lot of traveling, but I didn't mind. I knew I was doing what God wanted me to do. He kept expanding my roles and responsibilities, and I kept saying yes. It wasn't always easy, though. I once drove my old Chevy Corsica sixteen hours from Chicago to Wichita, Kansas, for a special youth service. I was working two jobs to support my new family, and being away was challenging. The youth leader had invited several local churches and assured me that there would be hundreds of kids at this event, all expecting to hear God's Word preached and to experience a fresh encounter with his Spirit.

When I arrived, though, I found only eighteen young people there. I was surprised, and maybe a little disappointed, but I was grateful for these eighteen kids who showed up. I preached my heart out to them as if there were eighteen hundred kids! I was grateful for the offering they collected for me, which totaled $17.43. That was about a fifth of what I'd spent on gas to get there. This was not the offering I was expecting, but it was truly okay because I wasn't there to stroke my ego by speaking in front of hundreds of people or to make money. I was there to serve God, to relish the more that he had given me, and to do my best for him. I was obediently exercising my faith in response to my calling, believing "whoever can be trusted with very little can also be trusted with much" (Luke 16:10).

Through the Roof

That role as youth president wasn't all that God had for me, either. In 1998 my father-in-law said he planned to retire soon and told me that he wanted me to become the pastor of our little church. I really had no interest. When I discussed her father's offer with Elizabeth, she agreed with me. While she loved her parents dearly, she had witnessed firsthand the challenges a pastor and his family often faced and had no desire for us to experience them. I was working in a jewelry store and had my sights set on becoming a state trooper. I turned down my father-in-law's offer, but still he persisted—he was just as stubborn with me as I had been with him when I was dating his daughter.

Finally, he convinced me to at least allow the church to vote on whether I should fill the role of pastor for them, and I agreed. Our church only had sixty-eight members, and I told God that if this was indeed what he wanted me to do, then I wanted every one of those sixty-eight people to vote for me. If only sixty-seven voted, then I could turn down the pastorate and feel fine about it.

All sixty-eight showed up, and they unanimously chose me to be their new pastor.

I accepted.

I was tempted to believe that, at last, I had arrived into the role for which God had chosen and marked me all those years before. But I also had a different perspective on God after all that I had seen him do in my life and in the lives of others. I was finally clued in to the fact that God's more doesn't end. As long as I continued being willing to follow him, trust him, and serve him, he would continue to move me progressively into more expansive roles.

In 2013, when I was featured on the cover of *TIME Magazine*, I finally realized that not only does God's more never end, but it also has no ceiling. God loves to blow the roof off of our expectations! How that cover story happened is still a mystery to me; once more, it was something that God clearly orchestrated. I didn't seek out that reporter, nor did anyone from our church or my team. Since that story ran, I continue to be amazed at the people, places, and events that God brings into my life. All I know is that I just keep saying yes, and God keeps providing more.

> *I finally realized that not only does God's more never end, but it also has no ceiling.*

I didn't have to say yes. Anywhere along the way, I could have said no, passively "waited on the Lord" until the opportunity closed, or chosen to go my own direction. But I knew in my heart that if I didn't say yes to God, I would miss out on something extraordinary—something far greater, more meaningful, and more satisfying than anything I could ever accomplish on my own. Now I'm like a kid on Christmas morning. I'm simply excited to see what present God will unwrap for me next.

Getting in Step

My life is far from perfect, but I continue to wonder why so many people resign themselves to less than God's best for their lives. Why settle for less when you can have so much more? I realize it's not that simple in the midst of all that life throws at you.

When the bills have to be paid and the kids need clothes for school and your boss is cutting your hours at work, it's hard to trust God for his more. When your spouse is diagnosed with cancer and the outcome is uncertain, it's tough to cling to God's promises. When you're battling a secret addiction and reluctant to make yourself vulnerable and get help, it's difficult to imagine how much more God has waiting for you. So you begin wondering what you should do and how to handle it.

If you're like me, you start to worry and then to feel desperate. You want to keep the faith, but you also want security and to take control of the future. Pretty soon you're stepping away from God, focused more on making things happen for yourself than on waiting on his timing or saying yes to the unknown door he is calling you to walk through. You may not even realize that you're no longer in step with God's Spirit. Like dance partners listening to different music, you are out of sync with God. You create your own melody, your own moves.

Or maybe you feel stuck in a rut, caught up in routines that leave you feeling like there will never be anything more. You love God, but your relationship with him has grown stale. You feel dizzy from all the pushing and pulling of life's demands, and stilling yourself before God is a challenge. You long for God's peace, for a sense of joy that you once had, for that sense of fulfillment that you taste when you're doing what you know God made you to do.

Regardless of where you are with God right now, he is waiting on you. He still has more for you. He hasn't given up on you, and it's not too late. When you invited Jesus into your life, you said yes to the more of God. Your Father marked you in that moment and sealed you with his Holy Spirit. You belong to him, and nothing can snatch you away. No matter how hard life may squeeze you, you will not break.

You are marked for more, my friend.

God has promised and planned a richer, more abundant life than the one you're living now. Will you trust him to reveal it? Will you give up your status quo to experience an abundance of life like you've never experienced? Jesus said, "Whoever finds their life will lose it, and whoever loses their life for my sake will find it" (Matt. 10:39). If you're willing to follow God, if you're willing to be led by his Spirit, then you can count on the fact that he always has more in store for you.

PRAYING FOR MORE

To experience God's more, we must continually rely on him—not ourselves, not other people, not the church. All aspects of our lives, including our worship, our walk, and our work should reflect our commitment to God as our heart's focus. Many people say they want more of God in their lives but aren't willing to practice the disciplines required to grow closer to him.

At the end of each chapter, I will encourage you to spend some time in prayer, asking God to show you the areas of your life that need work before you can experience his more. I'll provide a model for how you can begin "Praying for More," but please make it your own. There are no magic words, so just speak to God honestly and openly from your heart.

God, you know where I am right now, and we both know it's not where I want to be. Thank you for sending your Son to die on a cross so that my sins can be forgiven. Thank you for the gift of your Holy Spirit that you have used to mark me as your new creation and to seal me as belonging to you. Lord, I want to live in the more of you and the less of me. Show me where you want me to go now. I'm willing to follow you and to say yes to the more you're about to reveal. Amen.

Chapter 2

CALLED FOR MORE

The place God calls you to is the place where your
deep gladness and the world's deep hunger meet.
—FREDERICK BUECHNER

Before I became a pastor, I worked at a number of different jobs—fast-food restaurant manager, department store manager, and jeweler, to name a few. Each had its ups and downs, but working in a jewelry store provided great training in the psychology of sales. The way I got the job was by selling chocolates.

I was working at a clothing store part-time, and our church youth group was raising funds for summer camp by selling chocolates. Every day I went to work with my boxes of chocolates, and I would hit all the surrounding stores, including this jewelry store. Day after day I sold these chocolates to the same sweet-toothed employees. After a few days of watching me sell candy to his employees, the jewelry store manager approached me and said, "If you can sell diamonds the way you sell chocolates, I'll give you a job."

I took the job. Years later the owners of the company, a husband and wife team, visited our store. They were in the middle of a dispute, trying to figure out what to do with an expensive, gaudy cocktail ring that they were having trouble selling. The wife wanted to break up the ring and create many different pieces with its various diamonds, but her husband insisted it would be much more profitable if sold as one piece. He challenged me to sell it in thirty days, and I accepted. His only advice was to show it to everyone, and this I took to heart. I quickly discovered I had my work cut out for me. This piece of bling was so large and flashy that style-conscious customers didn't want it. And it was so high priced that fashion risk takers couldn't afford it.

A good salesperson always looks for the silver lining, or in this case, the solid fourteen-karat gold setting. At first I thought about the attributes of the ring—it was big, sparkly, and unique—and I looked for customers who would find those traits appealing. But then I realized another lesson from watching our clientele: don't assume which customers could or couldn't afford our merchandise based on their appearance. For instance, a young man came into our store one day in a pair of dirty coveralls. With grease under his fingernails from the carburetor he'd probably just finished repairing, he picked out a ladies' Movado watch. He paid for the watch with an elite black American Express card. On the other hand, we had women wearing designer dresses and gold rings whose credit cards were declined.

So I learned to appreciate the owner's advice. I decided I was going to show this expensive-but-gaudy ring to every customer who came into our store, no matter their reason for coming in. If a young couple asked to see engagement rings, I fulfilled their request but also showed them the ring. If a woman wanted diamond earrings, I said, "Forgive me, but I can't help but also show you this beautiful ring we have—and the price is lower than it's ever been!" Even when a janitor from a nearby building came in for a new watch battery, I got out the ring and talked it up.

Within a few weeks, that ring sold! If I had waited for the "perfect" customer, I might never have sold it. I knew that by showing it to each and every customer, I greatly increased the probability that it would sell. Plus, showing it to customers every day, usually several times a day, allowed me to practice my sales pitch and come up with new, creative ways to describe this piece of jewelry in the best possible light.

Good practice for answering the calling God had placed on my life.

Packed with Purpose

I went from selling expensive accessories to giving away God's priceless gift. I didn't know it in the jewelry store, but in addition to the way God marked my life for more, he had also called me to more. After I had given my life to him and been sealed by the indwelling of the Holy Spirit, I wanted to give everything I had to serve God's kingdom.

While I didn't think I had much to offer—certainly not money or material resources—I came to realize that God simply wanted all of who he had made me to be. He knew me when I was in my mother's womb and designed me with unique talents, personal strengths, and special abilities. Once I accepted the free gift of salvation through Christ, I discovered that these same talents, strengths, and abilities uniquely qualified me to answer the calling God placed on my life. He *marked* me with his Spirit when I invited him into my life; he *called* me to fulfill my purpose by serving him with all that he had already given me.

I compared our being marked by God to the way a suitcase gets tagged to identify its owner and its destination. But only when that suitcase gets opened and unpacked will its contents fulfill their purpose. *Marked* for more is like having that label that identifies the owner and indicates the destination. *Called* for more is unpacking your suitcase and living out of what's inside, using all the resources God has packed into you for his purposes of furthering his kingdom.

Here's another way to think about this distinction between being marked and being called. When I worked at the jewelry store, customers would occasionally pick out an expensive item—say, an engagement ring—and make a down payment on it. They would continue to pay on it over time, and then when they were ready to pop the big question, they would make the final payment and take full possession of the ring. Their down payment meant that ring was marked "sold" and no one else could buy it. But the ring hadn't served its purpose yet. Only when given and received as a symbol of a couple's loving engagement would it fulfill the purpose for which it had been designed.

I never wanted to be a pastor and was very reluctant to enter into full-time ministry. I didn't think I had what's required to be a good pastor. I wasn't a quiet, gentle, studious type who loved talking to people about the deepest, most vulnerable parts of their lives. And I wasn't a loud, outgoing type who loved being in front of people and managing a church and all its ministries. Okay, maybe I'm more of the latter than the former. Still, at the time my father-in-law asked me to take over our little church from him, I didn't see myself fitting the mold.

Yet it became clearer and clearer that this was what God was calling me to do. I didn't have to fit a certain mold or look like what I thought the pastor of New Life Covenant Church should look like. I only had to answer God's call by being available. And as it has turned out, God had been preparing me all along. If I hadn't trusted him, I might have missed the more he was calling me to experience.

> *If I hadn't trusted him, I might have missed the more he was calling me to experience.*

Bait Your Hook

When Jesus began his public ministry, he sought out followers willing to devote their time, energy, resources, and attention to him. We don't know much about the details, but there was apparently something so special about Jesus on the seashore that day, something so compelling, that fishermen *in the middle of doing their jobs* were willing to walk away *right then.*

> As Jesus walked beside the Sea of Galilee, he saw Simon and his brother Andrew casting a net into the lake, for they were fishermen. "Come, follow me," Jesus said, "and I will send you out to fish for people." At once they left their nets and followed him.
>
> When he had gone a little farther, he saw James son

of Zebedee and his brother John in a boat, preparing their nets. Without delay he called them, and they left their father Zebedee in the boat with the hired men and followed him. (Mark 1:16–20)

We cannot help being amazed and impressed with the immediate and radical commitment Jesus inspired in these fishermen. Notice that these four fishermen didn't hesitate, didn't ask about wages, and didn't say, "Let me think about it and get back to you." They immediately dropped what they were doing and committed themselves and their lives to following Christ.

We are not only called to leave our old lives behind in the same way but we must also be willing to fulfill the purpose Jesus gives us. This purpose is the same one he had: "to seek and to save the lost" (Luke 19:10). Just as Jesus called his original disciples to leave fishing behind and become "fishers of people," we are called to do the same.

You see, Jesus doesn't call us to a casual relationship; he calls us to follow him. This means that we yield to his leadership in our lives and cultivate a consistent and growing relationship. Simon and Andrew, James and John knew that Jesus wasn't calling them to be spectators. Jesus wanted them to join him to proclaim the good news. And to help explain his call on their lives, Jesus used his first followers' vocation as a metaphor for their new role. Jesus wants you, like his first disciples, to fish, to bring men and women into the kingdom of God.

But if you're going to fish for people, you have to enjoy it. It's not supposed to be frustrating, something you dread. Fishing is telling your story, living it out for others to see. Most of the fishermen I know exaggerate about the size of the fish they caught or "the one that got away." However, the kind of fishing to which Jesus calls us is about telling the ultimate truth.

With our words, actions, and attitude, it's saying, "Hey, at one time I was down here, but since God rescued me, I'm up here. Jesus died for me so that I can have new life—an abundant life, a wild, free, full-of-joy life." It's saying, "He died for me and he rose for me, and if he did it for me, he can do it for you."

So if fishing is simply telling others what Jesus has done in your life, then how do you bait your hook? By caring. The best bait addresses the needs in the lives of others. It's simply recognizing the needs, on all levels, of those around you and showing that you care about them and their needs.

So many people ask me how our church has developed so many different ministries. "What was your master plan?" they ask. "How did you decide which ministries to begin first?" And I always smile and tell them that the only master plan I have is the Master's plan. We simply looked for the needs in our community and connected them to people who have a passion for meeting those needs.

We've never started a ministry without having people in our church and on our team who feel called. Whether it's for our annual events like Hopefest (our back-to-school event), or ongoing ministries for the homeless, for survivors of abuse, or for at-risk kids—whatever the need—we try to meet it by caring. That's the best bait to use when you're fishing for people and reeling them into God's kingdom.

We value caring to the point that we train our deacons to care. Obviously we can't *force* them to care about someone they don't—but if we have to force them to care, then they probably shouldn't be a deacon! When we train them, we help them to listen and know how to respond. We remind them of spiritual priorities and the necessity of being willing to sacrifice in small ways and in large ones. You never know what will strike a chord with someone and lead them to the Lord.

We can't fix every problem or snap our fingers and fill every need. But we can always care. We can always give the way Jesus gave—unconditionally, sacrificially, compassionately. He calls us to follow him and to fish for others. That's the secret to unpacking all that God has for you as you answer his calling on your life.

Straight to the Source

The best example of someone who was called for more and constantly lived out of the more God had for him was Paul. If he was a fisher of people, then he caught some whoppers! His story amazes and inspires me. When I think I can't do something or I have to do something I don't want to do, I remember Paul and go back and read his writings again.

In a dramatic encounter with Christ on the road to Damascus, Paul was marked by God for more and forever changed. God also called Paul to be the apostle to the Gentiles and to spread the gospel beyond Israel to all the world, just as Jesus told his disciples to do in the Great Commission (Matt. 28:18–20). Paul directly addressed this process of being marked and called by God:

> I want you to know, brothers and sisters, that the gospel
> I preached is not of human origin. I did not receive it

from any man, nor was I taught it; rather, I received it by revelation from Jesus Christ.

For you have heard of my previous way of life in Judaism, how intensely I persecuted the church of God and tried to destroy it. I was advancing in Judaism beyond many of my own age among my people and was extremely zealous for the traditions of my fathers. But when God, who set me apart from my mother's womb and called me by his grace, was pleased to reveal his Son in me so that I might preach him among the Gentiles, my immediate response was not to consult any human being. (Gal. 1:11–16)

Notice the way Paul described this major transformation in his life. First, he wanted to make sure everyone ("brothers and sisters") knew that the gospel he preached did not come from other people—not Jesus's prior disciples, not Paul's parents, not someone he met in his travels. No other human source was involved—he received his calling to preach the gospel directly from Jesus Christ. Can you imagine that you're sitting at the kitchen table, the way my kids used to gather to do homework, and Jesus is there sitting across from you? Just you and Jesus as he tutors you in all you need to know about the gospel.

Paul knew that his listeners and readers might freak out a bit at this revelation, and he anticipated their concern. He knew the gossip going around about him and his past—how could he not expect people to talk? Paul said it was true: he was such a good student of Judaism and so passionate about his ancestral faith that he used to persecute and even kill followers of Christ.

So what changed? How did Paul go from being a hater of the church to being a loving follower of Jesus? Paul had a direct encounter with the living God. He reveals that this dramatic change happened to him by the power and timing of God, "who set me apart from my mother's womb and called me by his grace." Even before Paul was born, God had set him apart and then called Paul by his grace. Why? To reveal God's Son and to preach the gospel.

This isn't true only for Paul. All of us who put our trust in God as followers of Christ are set apart. When you're marked for more, God's Spirit is in you. When you're called for more, Jesus is revealed in how you live. God is inside us transforming us so that other people can see God through what we think, say, and do. When God lives in you, you walk like he walks, you talk like he talks, and you treat others the same way he treats you.

When you're called for more, Jesus is revealed in how you live.

In a sense, all of us have the same calling from God—to make Jesus known in all that we are and through all that we do—even though we live it out in all kinds of unique, diverse, wonderful ways.

Blinded by the Light

In case you're missing what a sharp contrast Paul makes between who he used to be and who he had become in Christ, let me provide some color commentary. Paul had an impressive résumé in his role as a by-the-rules Jewish religious guy. He had a solid upbringing from a good family. He was circumcised on the eighth day. He was of the stock of Israel. He was of the tribe of

Benjamin. He was a Hebrew of Hebrews. He had education. He was a teacher of the Law, the Torah.

Throughout his life, Paul (then known as Saul) maintained a spotless track record within the cultural religious system he practiced. In his traditional Jewish religion, righteousness could be achieved only by adhering strictly to God's law. Saul considered himself blameless and righteous because of how hard he worked to follow all the commandments and obey all the rules. He felt totally justified in his persecution of those radicals who were going around talking about grace and forgiveness in the name of Jesus Christ, whom Saul considered a criminal heretic. But his encounter with Jesus stopped him in his tracks—literally:

> Meanwhile, Saul was still breathing out murderous threats against the Lord's disciples. He went to the high priest and asked him for letters to the synagogues in Damascus, so that if he found any there who belonged to the Way, whether men or women, he might take them as prisoners to Jerusalem. As he neared Damascus on his journey, suddenly a light from heaven flashed around him. He fell to the ground and heard a voice say to him, "Saul, Saul, why do you persecute me?"
>
> "Who are you, Lord?" Saul asked.
>
> "I am Jesus, whom you are persecuting," he replied. "Now get up and go into the city, and you will be told what you must do." (Acts 9:1–6)

Saul asked the Jewish high priest for the authority to hunt down followers of "the Way" and kill them if necessary.

He would do whatever it took to make them stop preaching their gospel of grace, which contradicted everything Saul and the old Jewish religious order believed. Saul was convinced that the only way to God was through adherence to God's law. But then on his journey, Saul fell to the ground as the heavens opened to reveal a blinding light and a voice saying, "Saul, Saul, why do you persecute me?"

Nowhere in the Bible do we find Saul having any kind of encounter with Jesus before Christ's crucifixion and resurrection. Saul never met Jesus while Christ walked the earth, and yet Jesus indicated that this business of persecuting Christians was personal: *If you persecute my followers, my church, then you're perse-cuting me.* The same holds true for us today. Jesus told us, "If the world hates you, keep in mind that it hated me first. . . . If they persecuted me, they will persecute you also" (John 15:18, 20).

So don't be surprised when somebody attacks you because you're a Christian, a follower of Jesus. Our Savior told us this would happen. People committed to the ways of the world hate Jesus and therefore hate us because his Spirit lives in us. Their hatred can take all kinds of forms, and I've faced most of them. Certain political figures in our city have opposed the work of our church. Gangs have tried to intimidate me for not following their "rules." Voodoo practitioners in our neighborhood have cast spells and left mutilated chicken carcasses on our steps.

No matter what kind of persecution I've faced, I haven't backed down, because I know I have God's power dwelling in me. As long as I'm doing what he has called me to do, then I know he will empower me to do it. He will provide the resources so that you and I may bring his light into the darkness of the world around us. Years later—twenty-three years later, to be exact—Paul, imprisoned for preaching the gospel, shared his testimony with Governor Festus and King Agrippa and told them what Jesus told him that day on the road to Damascus:

> "Now get up and stand on your feet. I have appeared to you to appoint you as a servant and as a witness of what you have seen and will see of me. I will rescue you from your own people and from the Gentiles. I am sending you to them to open their eyes and turn them from darkness to light, and from the power of Satan to God, so that they may receive forgiveness of sins and a place among those who are sanctified by faith in me." (Acts 26:16–18)

Paul considered himself blameless until he met Jesus. Then he realized that none of us can follow God's law perfectly and save ourselves. That's why God sent his Son to die on the cross—because we could not pay the price, because he loved us so much. "For God so loved the world . . ." (John 3:16). Paul moved from life in the law to life in the Spirit. He learned to live by grace instead of works, to extend grace instead of holding people captive in legalism. He learned to let go of who he had been to become who God made him to be.

Free Radicals

Paul was a Christian killer. But before he was a Christian killer, before he was even born, God called him. No matter your age or where you are in life, you've probably made some mistakes and experienced some failures along the way.

We fixate on these wrong choices and missteps and label ourselves accordingly. We're failures. We make mistakes. We do sinful things. We have done things that have been very embarrassing. We have hurt other people. And so we perceive ourselves through the lens of how we've been wounded and how we wound others. But God doesn't look at our wounds. Just as he did with Paul, God looked at you in your mother's womb and called you to more. And his call is irrevocable; once he calls you, there's no turning back.

Paul never doubted that his life had been changed. He could easily have questioned, *How is that possible? What changed inside me? I don't understand,* but he didn't. He simply accepted his face-to-face encounter with Jesus for what it was, spiritual and supernatural. Paul didn't get to spend three years like the disciples did, following Jesus as he preached and healed the sick and forgave people's sins. Paul just had a crash—*boom!*—and everything was changed.

Paul's example encourages us, especially when we're tempted to focus on our mistakes. Because Paul evidently made a lot of them—even murdering innocent people just because they were following Jesus instead of the Torah. God still used him. Perhaps the dramatic change in Paul after he met Jesus on the road to Damascus explains why Paul was such a radical character. He had been set free to become who God called him to be. Paul faced about everything a person can face as he fulfilled his calling: shipwrecks, arrests, beatings, jail time, and earthquakes. And yet Paul wrote roughly half of the New Testament and converted countless men, women, and children to the Christian faith.

No matter what you've been through, how you've failed or

hurt others, how you've suffered or been hurt by others, God wants to use you for his kingdom. He has marked you for more, and he has called you for more. But he still gives you free will to choose how you will answer him. Will you live with the bold freedom and radical attitude of a Paul? Or will you put God's call on hold in your life?

Go Fish

God hasn't called you to fish for others because of how good you are or how good looking, how much money you have or how many degrees hang on your wall. The people Jesus called to be his disciples were common laborers, uneducated and inexperienced. They didn't have any theological credentials or status in the world. They didn't go to Bible school or have special training. They were fishermen, tax collectors, average people like you and me. Jesus met them at their labor, as a common man. Whatever your profession is right now, God is calling you to use it for his kingdom. The disciples were chosen by Jesus not for who they were but for what God could do through them.

It's not who you are. It's what Jesus can do through you if you will let him.

Will you accept the invitation and say, "Jesus, here I am, use me?"

At the root of it, Christianity is about following Jesus and fishing for those who need him. He uses

> *It's not who you are. It's what Jesus can do through you if you will let him.*

all that we are, all that we were before we met him, and empowers us to do more than we could ever do alone. There's someone who needs to be set free from darkness that only you can help. There's someone in pain who is going through something God has already brought you through. No one can reach that person better than you.

Don't be afraid. *Fish.* Share your story fearlessly. Others need to be saved. And they need to have their sins forgiven. You may be the only person willing to see their heartaches and needs.

And someday, when we get to heaven, when they see you there, they're going to say, "Thank you. Thank you for that one day when you spoke to me. Thank you for that one moment that you wouldn't let me push you away, and you stopped and talked to me about your life and about Jesus. Because you cared, I was removed out of darkness and stepped into the light. The power of Satan was broken from me, and I received God's forgiveness for my sins and accepted his power in my life. Thank you for fishing."

Let me leave you with a scene from a story I once read in which the writer imagined Jesus reentering heaven. As the angels talked with him, Gabriel noticed that Jesus bore the marks of the cross, and said to Jesus, "Master, you must have suffered terribly for those people down there."

Jesus said, "Yes, there was some suffering."

"And," said Gabriel, "do all of them know how much you love them? Do all of them know what you did for them?"

"Oh, no, not yet. Just a few people in Palestine know."

"So, what have you done," said Gabriel, "to let everyone know?"

Jesus said, "Well, I've asked Peter, James, and John, and a few others to tell others about me, and the others to tell yet others, and more and more, until the whole world has heard what I've done."

Gabriel was less than convinced that this was a workable plan. He said to Jesus, "What if Peter, James and John, and these other followers get tired and fail? What would happen if many years from now people do not tell others about what you have done for them? Do you have a contingency plan? Is there a backup strategy?"

Jesus smiled and said, "I have no other plan. I'm counting on them."

He is counting on you and me to fulfill our calling by casting our lines for people's souls. There is no other plan for how they will know God or get to heaven. So don't let fear stop you from giving your heart, your hands, your time to those around you. Don't let your concerns about what others might think slow you down from living out your calling.

So often you let fear stop you from going fishing: fear of being ridiculed, fear that you'll no longer be the most popular person in the room; fear that you'll be unfriended. That's why Jesus says, "Take courage! It is I. Don't be afraid" (Matt 14:27). Answering his call means following in his footsteps even when we can't always see what's ahead.

In the same way that Jesus called his first disciples, he is calling you and me to do more. People are desperate to come out of the dark into the light, to know true forgiveness and freedom. They are being oppressed by the power of the world, by the forces of the Enemy. They have to be set free from the power of Satan so they can experience the grace of God and be set free from the power of sin in their lives.

How is that going to happen unless you go fish?

Love is what calls you to do what you do. Your love for God motivates, sustains, and empowers you to step out of your comfort zone and fish in deep waters. If you truly want more of God in your life, open your heart as you answer his calling.

PRAYING FOR MORE

Father, I know you're not a respecter of persons. As you called Paul, as you called the disciples, you have also called me. Help me to respond to the call and fish for others. Allow me to put my fears aside and to step out in faith so that those in darkness may see your light. I want to follow in Jesus's footsteps and make loving others and leading them to you my life's singular focus. I want to use the many gifts, talents, and resources that you have given me to share the gospel with people and to advance your kingdom in the world. Help me to be sensitive to your Spirit within me and to follow your guidance in all that I do. Thank you, Lord, for calling me to more. I love you. Amen.

Chapter 3

LIVING IN THE MORE OF TODAY

I am only one, but still I am one. I cannot do every-thing, but still I can do something; and because I cannot do everything, I will not refuse to do something that I can do.

—HELEN KELLER

When I agreed to become a pastor, our church had sixty-eight members and an uncertain future. Started in the mid-1960s by the Reverend Ignacio Marrero, along with a faithful group of believers from the neighborhood, the church, then known as Palestine Christian Temple, met in homes until they could afford to rent a storefront. Over a decade later, the church had grown and finally purchased a permanent location right in the heart of Humboldt Park at 1665 North Mozart Street.

After thirty-five years, Reverend Marrero, who became my father-in-law, decided to retire and pass the mantle to me. That was almost twenty years ago. I had no idea what would happen;

I didn't know whether God would allow our little church to close, to survive by joining another congregation, or to thrive where we were in Chicago's gang-infested west side. On paper that last option seemed unlikely. The smart thing would have been for our congregation to sell our property and move to the safer, expansive suburbs.

But if you know anything about God, you probably know what I was learning: God's plans trump human logic every time. Many seeds of faith had been planted by my father-in-law and other devoted members, and God chose to bless their faithfulness shortly after my arrival. I cannot take credit for the growth we experienced. I figure the word must have gotten out: "You gotta come hear this guy, Choco! He's from the hood and tells it like it is." I had street cred.

It takes more than a pastor's reputation as a follower of Jesus for a church to grow. I could never have imagined what God had in store or what we would do once we outgrew our small facility. I simply knew he had entrusted me to shepherd and lead his church for him. I had no long-term vision to lead a megachurch with multiple campuses and a dozen community outreach ministries. I knew just enough to keep going, keep risking, to take the next step and make the next leap of faith, moment by moment.

I was learning to live in the more of today.

What Is That in Your Hand?

If I had stopped to think about what I was doing, I would have started doubting myself and quit on the spot. Like a mountain climber who does fine unless he decides to look down, I didn't know what I didn't know. I just kept following God's guidance and being obedient. If that sounds simplistic, it is—but that doesn't mean it was always easy.

There were times when I had my doubts and let the obstacles blind me from God's bigger picture. Like Moses, another reluctant leader, I sometimes became overwhelmed by what I lacked instead of grateful for what I had. But as we see with Moses, God always asks us to start where we are and use what we have:

> Moses answered [God], "What if they do not believe me or listen to me and say, 'The LORD did not appear to you'?"
>
> Then the LORD said to him, "What is that in your hand?"
>
> "A staff," he replied.
>
> The LORD said, "Throw it on the ground."
>
> Moses threw it on the ground and it became a snake, and he ran from it. Then the LORD said to him, "Reach out your hand and take it by the tail." So Moses reached out and took hold of the snake and it turned back into a staff in his hand. (Ex. 4:1–4)

Moses was a remarkable man who lived an amazing life. He was born to a poor Jewish family of slaves and raised by a princess as royalty in the king's palace. Moses then murdered an Egyptian, ran from the authorities, and lived as a fugitive in the desert. His story could have ended there, and Moses might have been happy if it had. Instead, he married the daughter of a Midianite priest, became a shepherd, and encountered Yahweh, the living God, in a burning bush. God had chosen Moses to deliver the Israelites from captivity.

Instead of getting excited or being honored to accept the Lord's call, Moses immediately unfolded a laundry list of excuses: "What if they [the elders and people of Israel] don't believe me? What if they don't listen to me? What if they don't follow me? And how will I ever be able to confront Pharaoh?" Moses was telling God, "Look, I'm having a really hard time believing that you're picking *me* to deliver the people. Why would you choose me? I'm a murderer. I'm a fugitive. I'm running from the authorities. And now you want to use me and give me more. But I don't even talk right. I stutter. I don't think I can do it, Lord!"

God always asks us to start where we are and use what we have.

But this was God he was talking to! The excuses I make before God never seem to hold up. I've learned it's better not even to try making excuses and just to step out in faith and move forward. God isn't interested in excuses—not Moses's, and not yours or mine.

God responded to the list of logical reasons why Moses was unable to lead his people. He asked Moses, *"What's that in your hand? What do you already have to work with?"* In typical God fashion, God answered a question with a question.

God wanted Moses to understand that he could get started with what he already had. He had no need to be a better speaker. No need to wait for people to accept him. No need to wait for the conditions to be right. No need to wait until the threat to his life was completely gone. No need to wait for anything. God told Moses, *"No waiting; you're ready right now!"*

This is the same message he tells you and me today.

There's no need to wait.

You have all you need.

You have God.

Hesitation = Limitation

God knew that Moses was afraid and hesitant. And God also knew that for Moses to move out of his fear and uncertainty, Moses would want reassurance. So God immediately provided a dramatic sign—can you imagine your walking stick turning into a snake before your very eyes?—and yet it wasn't enough to convince Moses. But once God began to reveal signs to answer Moses's question, the real problem came to light: *"Moses, it's not because you stutter. It's not because of the elders. It's because you don't want to go. It's because you're unwilling to trust me."*

When God gives you more, you must go.

If you want to live in the more of today, then you must obey *today*. Not when you have more proof, feel more prepared, or the weather changes. Right now. Keep in mind that when God gives us more and asks more of us, the situation may not be what we expect. In fact, it probably won't be what we expect at all.

> *When God gives you more, you must go.*

When I became the pastor of New Life Covenant in July 2000, I never expected to be where we are today. Now almost every day someone will ask me, "Did you ever think this would grow into a megachurch?" or "What was your strategy as you began starting new campuses around the greater Chicagoland area?" And I just have to smile and tell them, "I didn't even want to be a pastor! No, I had no idea. The only strategy I've ever tried to follow is the same one I follow today—listening to God's voice and following his directions."

I'm not perfect, far from it, and that's exactly why I've relied on God—because I knew I couldn't do what he kept asking me to do. When I feel totally insufficient, I remember that God is all-sufficient. In their burning bush conversation, God told Moses in effect, "Tell them I AM sent you" (see Ex. 3:14). Moses missed the point and focused on telling God, "But I am *not*."

Moses looked at himself instead of looking to God. If I look to myself, and if you look to yourself, we will never accomplish anything of eternal value and significance. So if you want to live in the more of today, then stop looking at your limitations, and look at the potential of God.

When we hesitate, we usually manage to complicate the situation. Every hesitation creates a new limitation. When God called me to lead this church, if I had hesitated, it would have created another limitation as my fears grew and my uncertainty multiplied. But all I had to do was walk in obedience, even if I couldn't always see where I was going. Sometimes you're not going to see the things of God in your life. You're just going to have to walk by faith and trust the Word of God.

> Every hesitation creates a new limitation.

If you are willing to step out in faith, God will honor your obedience and make you stronger. He wants you to face your past but to move forward. He is able to give you what you need to accomplish what he is calling you to do.

Something from Nothing

What God was asking Moses to do was huge! The Lord was asking him to face his past and to conquer his fears. Moses looked at himself, and he couldn't imagine doing what God was asking of him. Why? For the same reason we struggle to live in God's more today. We focus on our limitations instead of our Father's infinite resources. We focus on what we can't do instead of what he can do.

We put up excuses. We've barely taken our first steps before we start making excuses. By the time we become adults, we already have ten excuses why we're not where we're supposed to be. We say, "I can't do this. I don't have the money. I'm not smart enough. I don't have a degree. I'm too shy. I get too nervous. I'm not talented enough. Nobody's going to take me seriously."

Ever made any of those excuses? The greatest obstacle to living in God's more is not other people or difficult circumstances—it's ourselves. It's that voice inside all of us repeating the lies of the Enemy: "You can't do that—don't make a fool of yourself by trying! You know you're going to fail if you try that—and then what?" On and on, that false critic tries to take us out of the game just as God is putting us in.

We focus on our problems, our deficits, our conflicts, our barriers, our obstacles. *We're* the problem. God appeared to Moses in a burning bush and talked to him for crying out loud, and yet Moses still made excuses! He was thinking, *Wait, I can't do this.* He hesitated because he saw something was missing. He needed more confidence, more speaking ability. He needed more time to prepare, to train, to practice, as if forty years wasn't enough.

But Moses learned a vital secret to living in God's more: *God loves to make something out of nothing.* He loves to create his more out of our less. That's kind of his thing. I'm living proof! God took me, a Puerto Rican kid from an alcoholic, dysfunctional family in one of the roughest parts of one of the most dangerous cities in the country and made something of me. I failed third grade because I couldn't read, and you know what? By the grace of God, I now have completed not only a bachelor's degree but also a master's degree—and I'm working on a doctorate!

That's what God can do. I have worked hard and tried to be faithful in doing my part and obeying the Lord moment by moment, day by day. But God loves changing lives, doing what seems impossible to human beings, and drawing others to his love.

God did it with Moses, he has done it with me, and he can do it for you. I have no doubt that he has already started transforming you or you probably wouldn't be reading this book! *God is already at work in your life.* You are already in the midst of your more.

The question is not whether God can turn your nothing into his something. The question is whether you will stop making excuses long enough to look at what's in your hand. You have no need to want more, because God can use what you have already. God always has more—even as he requires more faith on our part to access it.

What do *you* have in *your* hand?

Give It All You've Got

After you let go of your excuses, you might still feel like you have nothing to give. But if you have Jesus, then you have everything to give. You may not always have what others want, but you always have what they need. Just as God calls us to use what is already in our hand, he also wants us to use it for his kingdom by serving others. In return, we're blessed with the fulfillment that comes from obeying God and living out our purpose.

Our faithfulness creates God's more in the moment. Here's how it happened with the first disciples:

One day Peter and John were going up to the temple at the time of prayer—at three in the afternoon. Now a man who was lame from birth was being carried to the temple gate called Beautiful, where he was put every day to beg from those going into the temple courts. When he saw Peter and John about to enter, he asked them for money. Peter looked straight at him, as did John. Then Peter said, "Look at us!" So the man gave them his attention, expecting to get something from them.

Then Peter said, "Silver or gold I do not have, but what I do have I give you. In the name of Jesus Christ of Nazareth, walk." (Acts 3:1–6)

Let me provide a little context and summarize the first two chapters of Acts. Jesus was crucified, died, and then returned to life. After individual encounters with their resurrected Master, the disciples were still uneasy about what it all meant and what would happen next. Then Jesus told them he had to go away but would send his Spirit to live inside them, to empower and guide and comfort them.

Following the Lord's instruction to wait in an upper room for this event, which we call Pentecost, the disciples gathered and waited ten days. Finally, they received the Holy Spirit, and he was a game changer. They received power—God's power to do more. More than they could even imagine! This is where our scene with Peter and John comes in. They had received the Holy Spirit at Pentecost and were now going to the temple.

Outside the temple, they encountered a man who had been lame since birth. This man probably survived by begging outside the temple gates. Maybe he had friends who would drop him off and then come back at the end of the day and help him get back home. So it was just another day of panhandling for this lame beggar when Peter and John came along. When he asked them for money, however, they told him they didn't have any money to give. Instead, they offered what they had— something far more valuable.

I can just imagine Peter saying, "Buddy, I know last week and the week before I gave you some change, but today my pockets are empty. And while I don't have any money, I'm happy to give you what I do have. In the name of Jesus of Nazareth, get up and walk!"

The reason why Peter and John specify Jesus Christ of Nazareth is because in those days, the name Jesus was common. Walking down the streets of Jerusalem, you might run into Jesus of Bethlehem, Jesus of Judea, and Jesus of Samaria. Peter and John, though, wanted to make sure that their Master, the one and only Jesus Christ of Nazareth, received the credit. He was their power source, the One enabling them to heal this man who had been lame since birth.

When you think about Peter and John and the lame man, compare what the beggar wanted with what he needed. He only asked for money. He didn't want healing or salvation. He didn't want liberation or transformation. He simply wanted cold hard cash. We do the same thing. We want to change, but we're only focusing on economic change—not on what we really need, which is a heart change.

Like the beggar with the disability, I used to think that money could solve my problems. I used to think that material things could solve almost any problem. But money only solves a temporary problem, not our constant need. We need Jesus along with everyone around us.

The disciples decided not to give what they normally would give, a coin or a concerned look. They decided, "We have this power now. We have Jesus inside of us. Let's give him that."

Sometimes when all you have is Jesus, Jesus is all you really need.

Elevation Revelation

Just as Peter and John offered what they had—Jesus—in response to the man's request, the beggar still had to receive the more they offered. It's crazy to think about him saying, "Uh, no thanks—if you guys don't have any cash, I'll just sit here. I don't really want to be healed. I'll just keep being lame." No one would say that, right? Even after God gives us more, we're often tempted to settle into a nice comfortable place. We become complacent and unwilling to exercise the more we have. We forget to give God the credit and praise for our more and leave the door open for our human pride.

Not the case, though, with our man with a disability. After he was healed, he began walking and jumping and praising God (see Acts 3:7–12). He was living proof of the power of Jesus

Christ. He couldn't contain himself and kept jumping around like a little kid! But God wasn't done with him yet. *With every elevation comes a new revelation.*

When God does more for us, we sometimes forget, and we take it for granted. And if we stay silent and don't voice our praise the moment we are presented with abundance, then we are tempted to believe that it was a coincidence. *Maybe I made that happen or maybe it happened because I deserved it.*

> With every elevation comes a new revelation.

What did Peter and John have? Jesus. What did the man with the disability have? Faith. And when Jesus and faith come together, something miraculous happens. When Peter extended his hand to the man, I wonder if he was remembering a similar scene that had taken place years before: Peter was sinking into a stormy sea and Jesus extended his hand and pulled Peter up. It's what we're all called to do—throw the same lifeline to others that was thrown to save us. Because the Lord rescued Peter, he was able to offer the same kind of healing in the name of the Lord.

All that was required of the man was to reach out. All that is required of us is to reach out to God. He is good to us and keeps all his promises. He has more for us than we can dream or even imagine. He can do what people say is impossible. I know because I've watched him do miraculous things for our church. When we outgrew the high school where we had been meeting for years, everyone around us said it was impossible to find a big enough facility in this part of Chicago, let alone enough affordable land, for us to relocate. When we found a parcel of land right in the middle of Humboldt Park where we could build, people said, "Choco, the church will never find a bank that will loan you that much money." Once our loan was secured—without a down payment, mind you—people said, "Getting the city of Chicago to give you the permit in less than nine months? Impossible." But with God's help and to his glory, we did it in three weeks. Come on! Can I get a witness? Somebody say, "Amen!"

Each step along the way, I was tempted to think the same thing—this is too hard, too big, too impossible. And every time, God made a way and did the seemingly impossible. Then the next opportunity for God's more revealed itself, and once again, I wondered, *Is this it? Have I reached the summit of what God has for me?*

I always used to think that every level was the culmination of God's more for my life, that this was it. But I have since learned that there's always more with God.

And here's the even better news: there is no ceiling with God! You have no idea what God is going to do in your life. Your mind cannot even conceive. Your ears have never heard. Your eyes haven't seen all that God has in store for you. When you walk in obedience to God, each new door will reveal even more! Your response to the more of God today will dictate how much more of God you have tomorrow.

I challenge you to do a little honest assessment right now. Where are you with God? Where are you with what God has already given you? What are you doing with it? What have you done today? How have you developed what God has given you?

Whatever is holding you back cannot prevent you from receiving God's more unless you let it. Imagine the guy with the disability by the temple door, every day when his friends dropped him off, thinking, *Is this it? I'm going to live like this for the rest of my life, a beggar? Guess I should be realistic and forget about my dreams. It's hard to chase a dream if you can't walk.* Then one day God sends him Peter and John, who say, "If you believe, grab our hands. Walk in the name of Jesus!" And the man's life changes in the blink of an eye.

I'm learning that to fully appreciate God's more, I need to be in a place of receiving God's more in my life. Moses had a staff in his hand. God said, *"I'll use that."* Maybe it doesn't seem like much to you, but God can use whatever you have in your hand. Maybe it's only a GED. God says, *"I'll use that."* Maybe you suffered from abuse growing up. God says, *"I can heal that."* Maybe you have a broken marriage or a secret addiction or a criminal past or something that feels impossible to escape. But God says, *"Trust me—I can use that. I'll heal you. Just take my hand."*

Will you let him?

Flight or Fight

If you want to live in the more of today, then you must make a choice to use what's in your hand, to give what you have, and to always trust God for more. The decision doesn't rely on your spouse or your kids, on your parents or your boss. You can settle for what you have or you can step out in faith with God for more. The decision to embrace God's more is yours and yours alone.

The importance of this choice reminds me of a story. One afternoon when an old man strolled through the park, he stopped to feed the pigeons, as he often did. But that day a group of teenagers saw the old man and began to taunt him. They called him names and threatened him, but the old man ignored them and kept feeding his beloved pigeons. Finally, one of the kids became determined to get the old man's attention, so he grabbed a pigeon from the sidewalk and put it behind his back.

"Old man," the kid said. "Is this pigeon behind my back alive or dead?"

The old man turned to look at him but didn't say anything.

The kid repeated his question. "What do you say, old man? Is the bird alive or dead back here?"

"That depends," the old man said, at last breaking his silence. "The answer to your question lies in your hand. You decide if the pigeon lives or dies. It's your choice."

More than a pigeon is at stake, my friend. You must decide whether to give flight to all that God has for you or to cling tightly and fight it because of your anger, fear, and doubt. Flight or fight—the choice is in your hands even as you read this on the page.

We're told, "God is able to bless you abundantly, so that in all things at all times, having all that you need, you will abound in every good work" (2 Cor. 9:8). Will you accept it? It may feel risky, but the greater risk is missing out on the wide-open adventure of faith God has for you. He has so much more for your future, for your marriage, your job, your family. Don't settle for less. Don't compromise your access to more by making excuses, hesitating, or thinking you have already arrived.

God has more for you today—and it starts *right now*!

PRAYING FOR MORE

Dear God, today I'm choosing to use what's in my hand and all the resources that you have already given me for your kingdom. I won't wait on more for the future while ignoring all you have blessed me with today. Give me your power, Lord, the kind of power that Peter and John used to heal the lame man at the temple gate. Allow me never to grow complacent and settle for less than your best. And remind me, God, that with you there are no limits on what you can do and how you can do it. I give my heart and all that I am to you, the great I AM. Thank you for loving me, saving me, and calling me to more today. Amen.

Chapter 4

PRECURSORS
TO MORE

*All of God's people are ordinary people who have
been made extraordinary by the purpose he has
given them.*

—OSWALD CHAMBERS

After I accepted the pastorate, it didn't take long for my
leadership to be tested. Ten months into my new role at
New Life Covenant Church, I faced a situation that my predecessor (my father-in-law) never encountered in thirty-five years
of ministry there. A youth volunteer on our team was caught
having sexual relations with a sixteen-year-old girl from our
congregation in a church van. Gossip spread quickly throughout our community.

Other team members, along with some of our elders and
members, urged me to say and do nothing. They hoped the
rumors would die, preventing further damage to the church's
reputation. This was a private matter, they stressed, and one

that should be handled within the church family. They wanted any conversations about what happened or discipline of the perpetrator to take place behind closed doors.

On the other end of the spectrum, I had neighbors and community leaders asking me how I was going to handle the situation. They were curious to see whether I would deny the stories they had heard and protect my own, or if I was willing to face the harsh consequences of telling the truth. For the people of Humboldt Park, it was a matter of trust and safety. After so much abuse and corruption had recently been exposed in the Catholic Church, my neighbors wanted to know how our children would be protected.

Despite the pressure from both sides, I knew what I had to do. God had placed me in a position of leadership within his church. I was responsible for making sure that all our members—especially our children and young people—were safe and secure. There was also a matter of the law. My team member was in a position of trust, and this young woman was a minor; this was statutory rape.

Confronting this young man was one of the hardest conversations I've ever had to have. He and his family had been part of our church for a long time and had many other friends and extended family in our congregation. While this young man tearfully confessed and apologized, he stressed that their interaction had been consensual. I told him that, in the eyes of the law, that didn't matter. He was an adult in a position of authority and trust; she was underage and within his care. I made it clear that if he didn't turn himself in, I would.

He agreed, but the situation got worse before it got better. At his hearing in the county courthouse downtown, the media got wind of it. WGN-TV was there covering the trial of a Chicago Bulls player charged with illegal possession of a firearm. Our case was called before the one for the Bulls player, and a reporter became curious. She began digging to find out the charges our volunteer faced. Suddenly the whole city and entire world knew all the details of the situation. Many people, both inside and outside our church, blamed me for dragging our church's name through the mud.

As painful, disappointing, frustrating, and heartbreaking as this incident was, I never second-guessed my decision. There was no way to please everyone in the midst of such a messy situation. But my job wasn't to please everyone or to protect the reputation of our church at the expense of the truth. My job was to maintain God's standards, including obedience to the law of the land. My job was to make our church a safe and secure environment where parents, grandparents, and community members knew their kids would be protected.

I learned that there is a price to be paid to experience God's more. You have to be committed to pleasing God rather than anyone else, you have to be faithful in serving the needs of others, and you have to remain humble and dependent on God. All of these point toward this truth: our primary currency in paying the price for God's more is faith.

The Cost of Worship

While God's grace is a free gift, our relationship with him has a cost. The Bible repeatedly makes it clear that the main way we grow in our relationship with him is through our faith, defined the Lord to reveal a direction and provide a facility for us—preferably much sooner! I kept trusting that God had more for us even if we had to go through an uncomfortable, inconvenient wilderness to find it.

The Pioneer and Perfecter

When we find ourselves in a wilderness, we get disoriented and stop doing what we know to do. That's the time when we need to cling to our faith the most. We need to be spending time with God in prayer, giving him thanks and praise, and studying his Word. Like the people of Israel, we often have short-term memories and lose sight of all that God has done for us. I suspect he allows us to continue to go through wilderness experiences so we keep learning how to trust him. Don't despise your wilderness, because your wilderness experience will increase your faith.

Unfortunately, these times of persevering to find the more that God has for you also leave you vulnerable to attacks from the Enemy. He wants to deter you from experiencing God's more. The enemy of your soul wants to plant seeds of doubt to interrupt your faith, seeds of confusion to keep you unfocused, and seeds of dissension to keep you isolated.

Our vulnerability during wilderness times explains why the Bible says in Hebrews to keep our eyes fixed on Jesus:

> Since we are surrounded by such a great cloud of witnesses, let us throw off everything that hinders and the sin that so easily entangles. And let us run with perseverance

as "the substance of things hoped for, the evidence of things not seen" (Heb. 11:1 NKJV). These two words—*substance* and *evidence*—provide the perfect, concise definition of biblical faith.

The word translated as "substance" literally means "to stand under" or "to support." Faith is to a Christian what a foundation is to a house. It holds you up; it gives you confidence. When you walk by faith, you grow stronger in this foundational "substance." The word translated here as "evidence" simply means "conviction." This is an inward conviction of belief we hold, trusting that what God has promised, he will perform.

> While God's grace is a free gift, our relationship with him has a cost.

This definition of faith begins a chapter in the New Testament, Hebrews 11, loaded with a list of heroes of faith. The writer of this passage was originally addressing a generation of Jewish people who insisted that the only way to know God and gain his favor was to work for it. This audience grew up observing ceremonies and making sacrifices, trying to be morally right by fulfilling every little detail of the Hebrew law.

But Jesus came to cut through all of those temporary methods once and for all. Through our belief in Christ, we have direct access to the Father. The writer of Hebrews stressed that the only way to know God and enjoy his favor is by faith and faith alone.

To illustrate his point, the writer then provided a who's who of the Old Testament and indicated how each one demonstrated their faith. Abel was commended for his *worship*. Adam and Eve had two sons, Cain and Abel. When God asked them both to present him with an offering, Abel gave his very best. Cain, however, gave halfheartedly. He was not motivated by the same desire to worship God through his offering. Abel was commended, and God acknowledged his worship, and Cain became outraged when God accepted his brother's offering but rejected his own.

Consequently, Cain murdered his brother. This story reminds us that other people will often feel threatened, jealous, or upset when we worship God completely and give him control over every area of our lives.

People may not like when you give more time and attention to God than to them. You're a risk factor when you're the one who gives more in your family. Abel risked standing out from his brother Cain and paid the price. Maybe Cain said to himself, *Who does my brother think he is? Does he think he's better than me? Well, I'll show him!*

When you place your complete faith in God and worship him as your number one priority, don't expect others to understand or to applaud you. More than likely, they will give you a hard time, talk about you behind your back, and reject you. When you establish the precursors for more in your life, you usually pay the price of losing certain friends and family members.

> *You're a risk factor when you're the one who gives more in your family.*

Jesus told us not to be surprised when the world hates us; in fact, we should expect it. "If the world hates you, keep in mind that it hated me first. If you belonged to the world, it would love you as its own. As it is, you do not belong to the world, but I have chosen you out of the world. That is why the world hates you" (John 15:18–19). It's human nature to want others to like us, but as the old saying goes, you can't please all of the people all of the time.

Deepening your faith in God requires you to put him first despite what others think. It wasn't easy for me to see a young volunteer I cared about face the consequences of his sin. Because I had committed to serve God, not people, I had to obey God. Many people challenged me, saying, "I thought your God was all about grace and forgiveness! Why can't you do the same?" I responded by stressing that even though God forgives us, we still have to face the consequences of our sinful choices and the impact our sin has on the lives of others. Yes, it would have been easier just to forgive and forget, but I would not have been obeying God's call to lead his church if I had chosen that path.

We limit what God is trying to do through us by trying to please everyone else. So many times we lose our identity when we let everyone else influence our decisions. We don't even know who we are because we're trying to please our spouse, our kids, our family. We lose sight of God's standards and his ways because we're focused on pleasing our boss, our coworkers, our friends, our neighbors. By pleasing people, however, we don't even know who we are or what we believe anymore.

When we live for God instead of doing what others want, they will notice and they will not be happy. I've seen people come to our church who used to be consumed by drugs and alcohol, going out to bars and clubs every night. They face a backlash from their family and friends when they invite Jesus into their lives. Suddenly the people who used to laugh at them, be embarrassed by them, or party with them, now hate them.

If you want to cultivate the kind of faith that can handle God's more, then you need to worship like Abel. No matter the cost.

Walking with God

The writer of Hebrews indicated another way we can deepen our faith like these saints in the Faith Hall of Fame. Just as Abel was commended for his worship, Enoch was commended for his *walk*. The Bible says Enoch walked with the Lord for three hundred years. The fact that our human lifespan is now less than a third of that amount makes it even harder to imagine what it must have been like for Enoch to enjoy that kind of daily intimacy with God.

But such deep fellowship has been God's desire for us all along. In Genesis we are told that Adam walked with God in the cool of the day before sin interrupted their relationship. From the time of Adam until Enoch, there were seven generations. God still wanted to walk with his creation, his beloved children.

Before you start thinking it was easier to walk with God in Enoch's day, let me remind you that he lived during one of the worst times in history. How do I know this? Because right after Enoch, the earth was flooded because the people were so wicked. If anything, Enoch may have had no support or encouragement from other people in pursuit of his relationship with God.

Nevertheless, Enoch walked with God his entire life, for three centuries. And keep in mind what it means to walk with someone. When you walk with someone, there's communication with that person, a closeness, synergy and harmony, mutual trust and enjoyment.

Ideally, this is the way a married couple travel together, side by side, reliant on each other and headed in the same direction. I must confess, this is not always easy to do. I remember a time when my wife, Elizabeth, and I went on a cruise vacation.

Our ship came to a port where we could go ashore and spend the day before returning that evening. So we took a cab to the beach and enjoyed the beautiful sunshine and the feel of the ocean breeze on our skin.

We spent most of the day there, and pretty soon it was time to head back to the ship. From the beach, we could see our ship up ahead of us, so I said, "Babe, let's just walk back. It'll be romantic. Let's just hold hands and keep walking on the beach." To add the perfect soundtrack for our little stroll, I then began to sing, "Let's take a walk together near the ocean shore," the beginning of Kool and the Gang's hit "Cherish." Thinking I was being terribly romantic, instead of being cheap for not wanting to take another cab, she agreed and we walked hand in hand. We were like a couple on a picture postcard.

That lasted about fifteen minutes.

Then we start walking faster and clenching each other's hand tighter. We were sweating in the tropical heat, getting sand in our shoes, and starting to get hungry. Still the cruise ship loomed in the distance, appearing no closer than when we started. After an hour, we dropped our hands and stopped speaking to each other, but still we kept on walking. Two hours went by. For the love of God, where was that boat? While we could see it, we still had a ways to go.

Finally, after two and a half hours, we arrived—tired, hungry, miserable, angry, and determined not to speak to each other. This was definitely *not* the kind of walking Enoch did with God. While Elizabeth and I can laugh about it now, it took a while for us to get to that point. For Enoch to walk with God for three hundred years, they must have had an amazing relationship!

If you want to cultivate the kind of faith Enoch had while walking with God, then I encourage you to consider who else you're walking alongside. In your desperation for having a boyfriend or a girlfriend, a husband or a wife, a best friend or a community, don't compromise God's standards. The Bible reminds us:

> Do not be yoked together with unbelievers. For what do righteousness and wickedness have in common? Or what fellowship can light have with darkness? What harmony is there between Christ and Belial? Or what does a believer have in common with an unbeliever? What agreement is there between the temple of God and idols? For we are the temple of the living God. As God has said:
>
> "I will live with them
>   and walk among them,
> and I will be their God,
>   and they will be my people." (2 Cor. 6:14–16)

So consider who your traveling companions are as you seek to walk with God, to trust him completely. Sometimes it's obvious that others don't share our commitment to Christ, and we can separate ourselves from them accordingly. But at other times it's more difficult. They may be family members or lifelong friends. We may have a lot of shared history. But if they're not walking with God with the same

If you want to cultivate the kind of faith Enoch had while walking with God, then I encourage you to consider who else you're walking alongside.

level of trust and commitment, then they may be preventing us from experiencing more.

If you want to strengthen your faith to receive God's more in your life, then you must walk with God daily. Cultivate your relationship with him and get to know him the way Enoch did, and I promise you will be ready for all the more you can handle.

Build Your Boat before It Rains

Abel was commended for his worship, Enoch for his walk, and next we're told Noah was commended for his *work*. All three of them had incredible faith in God, but I love the fact that Noah had to work long before the rains came. Noah had to choose whether to be obedient to God or to follow what his senses told him.

Long before there were any clouds in the sky, Noah chose to build. He didn't know when the rain would start falling or how long it would take to flood the earth. He simply knew he had to do what God told him to do. He was just obedient. He built despite the climate of his culture. Like Abel and Enoch and all the other Hall of Famers listed in Hebrews 11, Noah *acted* on his faith.

Stepping out in faith and taking action is often the hardest part of obeying God. But it's essential if we're to grow closer to him and to experience the more he has for us. You cannot say to the Lord, "Lord, I want a job. I've been sitting here on this sofa for four days." No, you're going to have to get up. You're going to have to knock on doors, and you're going to say, "Lord, I'm going to put myself out there. I'm going to put my résumé out there. I'm going to knock on every door, because getting from here to there requires action."

You can't just say, "I want my bachelor's degree," and have it show up in a box of Cap'n Crunch. No, you're going to have to go to school. You're going to have to make some sacrifices. You're going to have to work hard. You're going to have to persevere. You're going to have to build your boat before it rains.

If you want to be ready for God's more in your life, you're going to have to work. It's not given to you. You have to work. In today's culture there's a spirit of entitlement. We think, *I deserve this. I've already worked hard to get where I am. I shouldn't have to wait to get what I want now.*

Listen, you and I don't deserve anything! God is so gracious to bless us with his abundant gifts. But he still requires us to work for more. Whatever I have, I've worked for it. It took me seven years to get my bachelor's degree; for the last two years I traveled from Chicago to Deerfield, Illinois, every week battling with traffic and every inclination to just stay home. How many times did I want to quit? Every week. Every time I made that drive, every time I got up at 5:00 a.m. to do homework. Every time I sat stuck in traffic missing dinner with my family. I thought about quitting every week.

But I knew God wanted me to finish my degree. He had provided so much and opened the way where I never thought there would be one. Other people had invested their time, attention, and money in my education. I simply couldn't quit. So as soon as that thought popped into my head each week, I made sure I had my response ready: *No, Choco, you have to finish what you started. You're not quitting, not today.*

So much of being ready for God's more in your life is

refusing to quit. We will always face obstacles, delays, barriers, and disappointments in pursuit of moving forward in our faith. But like the many saints before us, we learn to keep our eyes on the Lord. We remember, like Abel, to give God our devoted worship, our very best. And like Enoch, we walk with the Lord step-by-step every day. And like Noah, we take action, doing the work required to fulfill the mission God has given us.

So much of being ready for God's more in your life is refusing to quit.

Do You Know Who I Am?

There's one other precursor to growing your faith and experiencing God's more that I must emphasize: humility. Our pride stands in the way of our heart being ready to handle God's more. We cling to our achievements, our possessions, our titles, and our self-importance when we should let go of them so we can receive something infinitely better that God wants to give us. Unfortunately, many of us learn this lesson the hard way.

When I think about the humility required to receive more, I think of a mission trip our church made a few years ago to the Dominican Republic. We had a large group fly down to minister to inhabitants in the rural village of La Bombita.

While we'd all been warned this ministry wasn't for the faint of heart, we still weren't prepared for the impoverished conditions. Villagers had no clean drinking water and no segregated sewage system. Along with the sweltering tropical heat and swarms of flies and mosquitoes, the stench of human waste and animal feces was overpowering. We had our work cut out for us, so I quickly divided our group into teams and assigned them various tasks, none of them particularly pleasant.

I didn't have time to stop and think about who I was assigning to which tasks, but I could tell pretty quickly that one of our team members was having a hard time. This young woman, Veronica, and her husband were fairly new to our church and to the Christian faith. I had been pleased but a little surprised when she signed up to join our trip because I knew she wasn't accustomed to such "hands on" ministry.

Veronica had quite an impressive résumé. In addition to being married to a highly respected and prominent elected official in Chicago, she worked for one of the most powerful congressmen in Illinois as his chief of staff. Highly efficient and keenly intelligent, Veronica had earned a master's degree in urban planning and public policy.

As it turned out, those were not the skills needed on our trip. Consequently, Veronica ended up on the team assigned to clean up a large field that had been used as a garbage dump. We had decided to transform it into a baseball field where children could play, separate from the new latrine we would also be digging. I remember Veronica looking at me funny and saying, "Wait—you want me to do what?"

Nonetheless, a few minutes later she donned gloves and a mask and began collecting trash, feces, and assorted debris. Her body language made it clear she wasn't happy, but her attitude seemed softened somewhat when many of the local children began helping. The contrast was striking: the kids making a game of the cleanup, laughing and singing, and poor Veronica barely able to keep standing in the midst of such filth.

I got busy with my own team's task, so it was several hours

before I saw her again. When I did, she gave me another funny look when she saw me knee-deep in empty pop bottles, used diapers, shredded cardboard, and other trash we were separating into a compostable landfill for the village. I didn't have time to stop and make sure she was okay and just had to pray she could keep going.

Toward the end of the trip, Veronica came to me and said, "I'm so sorry for my attitude at the beginning of this trip. I came feeling so important and just assumed I'd be placed in charge of overseeing some of the teams because of my administrative experience. So when you assigned me to clean up that nasty field, all I could think was, *Don't you know who I am! Seriously?* But then later that day, I saw you down in the landfill alongside everyone else. I realized that you didn't consider yourself too important to do the hard work that needed doing. Your example of humility caused my heart to break and made me spend a long time alone with God repenting of my self-absorbed attitude. Only after I yielded to him did I realize the incredible blessing I've received by being here."

Veronica's story reminds us that the more of God can be experienced in places and situations where we'd least expect to find them. She had a graduate degree, an important career, talent, money, and power—and yet she only experienced God's more when she put those aside. She learned that we need less of what we've been relying on to get by in life and more of what only God can give us. We have to decrease so that he can increase in our lives. But this requires a true servant's heart and humility.

Shortly after our missions trip, we asked Veronica to become chief of staff for me at the church. Her experience, expertise, and intelligence come into play every day and bless our entire church community in countless ways. And she remains one of the humblest people I know.

PRAYING FOR MORE

Lord, I truly want to walk with you just as Enoch did, to always give you my best just as Abel did, and to work diligently and obediently just as your servant Noah did. Draw me closer to you, Lord, so that I may be prepared and vigilant for the more you want to reveal in my life. Dissolve my pride and help me overcome the ways I seek the approval of others instead of pleasing you first. Thank you for the example of Jesus and the humility we see in his life. Let me serve others as he did and share the good news of the gospel with everyone around me. Empower me through your Spirit to live not for myself but only for you. Amen.

Chapter 5

DETERRENTS
TO MORE

A challenge only becomes an obstacle when you bow to it.
—RAY DAVIS

I 'm afraid I have some bad news, Pastor Choco," said the voice
on the other end of my phone. "Your church will have to find
somewhere else to meet for the summer. We're remodeling the
auditorium, and the whole building will be under construction
at least until September."

I sat stunned in my office. A spring thunderstorm drummed
rain against my window as gray clouds swirled overhead to
match my mood. Our church had been renting a school auditorium for our Sunday services for more than eight years. As
our membership continued to increase, I knew it would only be
a matter of time before we outgrew the auditorium, but I had
hoped to have a plan by then. Suddenly it looked as though we
would be forced to move, at least for several months, whether
we had a plan or not.

"Okay," I finally said to our administrative contact at the school, "thanks for letting me know. Can you recommend any other locations that could hold our congregation? Maybe another school?"

"Yes, I'd be happy to inquire and see if another school's auditorium is available. I'll get back to you as soon as I can find out."

Later that afternoon, the school property manager called me back and offered us another venue to rent for the summer. It would hold us, but unfortunately, it was in a different part of town and miles away from the heart of our community. I turned it down and thanked her for trying, frustrated by this turn of events. Already, I could hear members of our church criticizing me for not moving our congregation.

"We should have already moved the church out of Humboldt!" a number of people told me. "We're never going to find affordable property in this part of the city, so we might as well pack up and move."

Despite the logic of such a move, I had always felt God calling me to keep our church in the heart of the community where we were. I didn't think he wanted us to move now, but I needed a solution. I began praying several times throughout each day, asking God to guide us and make his will clear for our church's location. Our elders and other dedicated prayer warriors joined me, and we all concurred that God wanted us to stay in Humboldt Park. However, how and where we were going to stay still wasn't clear.

I knew God had more, but I also knew I needed more patience while I waited on him to reveal it.

A Way in the Wilderness

Often when we're walking with God in the fullness of his more, we reach a point that feels like a dead end. Whether it's an unexpected layoff, a betrayal by our spouse, the loss of a child to addiction, or a physical condition within our own bodies, we all face those moments where it feels like a brick wall has just dropped in front of us. Sometimes these obstacles are in our way because we've made a poor decision or failed to obey God. Other times it's the result of someone else's weakness or sinful choice. And other times life just happens.

At first these deterrents to more overwhelm us and leave us wondering why God would allow something like this to happen. Despite our uncertainty or frustration, we know that God always has a plan and has promised to remain with us and guide our steps. He has given us his Spirit to dwell in hearts and empower us, comfort us, and protect us. But sometimes we struggle for so long that we begin to wonder how to move forward. The urgency of the situation, such as when our church had to relocate, can leave us desperate for God's direction.

During these moments when I'm tempted to get discouraged, I remember how God allowed the people of Israel to remain enslaved in Egypt for more than four-hundred years. They prayed and waited and watched as generation after generation passed, and nothing seemed to change. Then, just when the odds seemed stacked against them, God raised up Pastor Moses to confront Pharaoh and lead the Israelites dramatically through the Red Sea.

Just imagine that moment: they had waited so long and had

overcome so much, and suddenly they were cornered and had
nowhere to go. Just as we're often prone to do, they panicked:

> "Didn't we say to you in Egypt, 'Leave us alone; let us
> serve the Egyptians'? It would have been better for us to
> serve the Egyptians than to die in the desert!"
>
> Moses answered the people, "Do not be afraid. Stand
> firm and you will see the deliverance the LORD will bring
> you today. The Egyptians you see today you will never
> see again. The LORD will fight for you; you need only to
> be still."
>
> Then the LORD said to Moses, "Why are you cry-
> ing out to me? Tell the Israelites to move on. Raise your
> staff and stretch out your hand over the sea to divide the
> water so that the Israelites can go through the sea on dry
> ground. . . ."
>
> Then Moses stretched out his hand over the sea, and
> all that night the LORD drove the sea back with a strong
> east wind and turned it into dry land. The waters were
> divided, and the Israelites went through the sea on dry
> ground, with a wall of water on their right and on their
> left. (Ex. 14:12–16, 21–22)

I love the response the Lord gave to Moses here after the
people of Israel began freaking out: "Why are you crying out
to me? Tell the Israelites to move on." It's almost as if he were
saying, *"Why are you waiting on me to do something when you just
need to keep going?"* Where the Israelites saw only water, God
knew there was dry land. They felt backed into a corner, but
God planned to use it as their escape hatch.

You would think that such a daring escape and last-minute rescue would have silenced any lingering doubts held by the people of Israel. Clearly, God had not forgotten them, and he delivered them from bondage in ways only he could orchestrate. However, the people started grumbling again once they realized that they still had to go through the wilderness before they could reach their new home, the promised land.

It just didn't seem to make sense to them. They had already endured so much and had overcome impossible obstacles—shouldn't their lives be easier? Wasn't there a shortcut they could take so they could get home faster?

Their questions, concerns, and frustrations were not so different from my own that spring when our church had to find a new meeting space. As the days gave way to weeks, we still had not been able to find a venue in our community that could hold us. I was losing patience and couldn't understand why God would put us in such a predicament. Faced with no viable spaces where we could hold services, I got inspired. We could hold our services in a huge tent in a nearby school yard, a throwback to old-time revival tent meetings from a bygone era.

Everyone in our congregation liked the idea—at least until we had one of Chicago's wettest, stormiest summers. Instead of a revival meeting, our outdoor space looked more like a mud pit at a monster truck rally! At this point I became even more frustrated and wondered if God didn't want us to hold services during the summer. Was I not hearing what he was trying to tell me?

Our church reminded me of the people of Israel wandering in the desert looking for the promised land. Remembering they had camped in the wilderness for forty years, I prayed for

the race marked out for us, fixing our eyes on Jesus, the pioneer and perfecter of faith. For the joy set before him he endured the cross, scorning its shame, and sat down at the right hand of the throne of God. Consider him who endured such opposition from sinners, so that you will not grow weary and lose heart. (Heb. 12:1–3)

Because Jesus was able to get through the suffering that ultimately landed him on the cross, he was able to fulfill his purpose in coming to earth. He sacrificed himself in our place, doing what we ourselves were unable to do because of our sin. Jesus endured all that was set before him to open the fullness of God's more for all of us.

Our hope is this: Jesus made it and showed us how we can make it too. We don't have to get sidelined by hindrances and entanglements, because he has already won the battle for us. Too many of us are sitting back and waiting for victory to happen when victory has already been placed on our life.

Stop waiting to walk into victory and begin to start walking *with* the victory you already have. Don't wait for victory: walk with victory, talk with victory, speak with victory, think with victory, because victory happened when Jesus died and was raised from the dead. The moment he conquered death, he conquered all.

> *Stop waiting to walk into victory and begin to start walking with the victory you already have.*

The Enemy is going to try to discourage you. He is doing all he can to prevent you from being you, from discovering your true purpose, and from building a legacy that is worth following. The Enemy doesn't care how successful you are at life. He doesn't care how much money you have in your bank account. He doesn't care how many properties you own. He doesn't care about your position or your title. He doesn't care about your health. He doesn't care whether you're physically fit or you're unhealthy. He doesn't care if you attend church.

Let me tell you what the Enemy does care about. He cares about distracting you from the truth of who you are in Christ. He is committed to leaving you spiritually bankrupt. He is determined to use anything and everything—your success as well as your struggles—to derail your faith.

He will use your money, your family, your career, your friends. He will use your life as a way to keep you busy with earthly endeavors so that you don't get the more of God. But we're not defenseless. We can take steps to discourage Satan and resist his snares. We're not his punching bag, left to take his blows and stay down for the count.

No, God has called us to more. Nothing the devil can throw at us can prevent us from experiencing all that our Father has for us. As Paul wrote to the Romans, "I am convinced that neither death nor life, neither angels nor demons, neither the present nor the future, nor any powers, neither height nor depth, nor anything else in all creation, will be able to separate us from the love of God that is in Christ Jesus our Lord" (Rom. 8:38–39).

How to Handle a Bully

When we're walking through the wilderness, we have three main weapons to empower us and to sustain our faith in the midst of the devil's snares. Think of them as deterrents to our deterrents, antidotes for the poisons the Enemy wants to use to take us out of the fight, keys for the locked corners where we find ourselves feeling trapped.

The first one is the most obvious and the most potent: the power of Jesus. Whenever we feel lost in the wilderness, we must remember that if we have Christ, we have everything. We have all that we need. Many times we gradually add caveats to the power we have in Christ. We end up thinking that we need Jesus and our church, Jesus and our pastor, Jesus and our small group, Jesus and enough money for the ministry we want to launch, Jesus and the place we're supposed to move.

But we don't need anyone or anything else to access the full power of God through his Son. We're told, "There is one God and one mediator between God and mankind, the man Christ Jesus, who gave himself as a ransom for all people" (1 Tim. 2:5–6). We must remind ourselves that we have his Holy Spirit within us at all times.

The devil tries to keep you distracted from relying on Jesus as the source of your power. He wants to distract you from worshiping and loving and serving Jesus. He understands that you have no authority without Christ. He knows that without Jesus—I don't care how successful you are—you have no authority. Because money can't buy you peace; money can't buy you joy; money can't buy you salvation. Only Jesus Christ can do any of that—and if you don't have him, you have no authority.

One example of Christ demonstrating his power over the Enemy took place when he was teaching on a Sabbath in a synagogue:

Then he went down to Capernaum, a town in Galilee, and on the Sabbath he taught the people. They were amazed at his teaching, because his words had authority.

In the synagogue there was a man possessed by a demon, an impure spirit. He cried out at the top of his voice, "Go away! What do you want with us, Jesus of Nazareth? Have you come to destroy us? I know who you are—the Holy One of God!"

"Be quiet!" Jesus said sternly. "Come out of him!" Then the demon threw the man down before them all and came out without injuring him.

All the people were amazed and said to each other, "What words these are! With authority and power he gives orders to impure spirits and they come out!" (Luke 4:31–36)

Notice how forcefully Jesus spoke and delivered this man of the impure spirit: "Be quiet! Come out of him!" He didn't waste time engaging in conversation with the demon or attempt to coax it out with nice language and a "pretty please." No! Like the mighty warrior he is, Christ demanded the impure spirit to leave this man based on Jesus's authority as the Son of God.

Sometimes when we're under attack, we act like the polite kids I remember from elementary school who tried to get the class bully to leave them alone. After ignoring the bully, they'd eventually say, "Stop bothering me. Please leave me alone. I'll tell the teacher if you don't stop." Meanwhile, the bully just laughed and kept teasing them because the bully knew he had the upper hand.

When the Enemy is trying to tempt us and trap us in one of

his snares, we can't tiptoe by him and apologize for not staying longer. Instead, we must call on the name of Jesus and use the same kind of forceful authority our Lord demonstrated in this scene. Notice what happened after Jesus called out the demon: the impure spirit fled and left the man alone without injuring him. And all the people watching were amazed and said, "What words these are! What power and authority!"

How many times have you said something but lacked power behind your words? Instead, it comes out tentative; your uncertainty and lack of confidence seep through your tone. This is not how God used words. God's spoken word is what created this world we live in.

When God said, "Let there be light," there were no questions in between. There were no what-ifs. When God separated the sky from the land, God said it, and it took place. Also, keep in mind that for someone to speak, that being has to have breath. The Bible says that God formed Adam, shaped him, constructed his bones, and put flesh on top of him. But still he had no life. It wasn't until God breathed into him that Adam had life.

God has breathed life into you, my friend. The breath of his Spirit is in you with the full force of his power and authority. Just like Jesus, who spoke the demon out with power and authority, you too have that ability and power. You too have that authority. The power is in your breath.

For the Bible says that life and death are in your tongue, your words. When you speak, what you speak will come into existence. You have the authority to tell the devil to shut up and back away from you. You don't need to sit back and take what the devil throws at you.

Open up your mouth and speak the promises of God found in his Word. Use your tongue and begin to speak what you know shall come to pass. You have the authority to speak for the things you hope for yet do not see. That is faith. The power is in your breath, through your words, because of Jesus. So when you're struggling in the wilderness, don't forget to call on God and use the full authority he has given you through his Son, Jesus Christ.

When you speak, what you speak will come into existence.

Worship in Your Worst

After the power of Jesus, the greatest deterrent to the Enemy's attacks is the power of your worship. If there's anything that discourages the Enemy, if there's anything that discourages Satan, if there's anything that discourages the demons in hell, it's when you're facing the worst of the wilderness and yet you still come before God and worship him. The Enemy hates this because he knows it's not logical—worshiping in the midst of the wilderness requires faith and demonstrates your trust in the Lord.

During those times when you're hurting but still choose to worship, I bet the devil's thinking, *Why are they worshiping in the midst of their suffering? It doesn't make sense! I thought I had them! They were stuck in shame over those stupid mistakes they made. They were so depressed over their chronic sickness. Weren't they flirting with the idea of suicide just yesterday, and now look at them, lifting up their hands and worshiping! I hate that! One minute they're gasping for breath, and the next they catch a second wind with a breath of fresh air.*

Nothing discourages the Enemy more than when he thought he had you, yet you worship God, saying, "Lord, I don't got it, but I know you do. I don't have the strength for it, but I know you do. I don't have the peace, but I know you do. I don't have the joy, but I know you do. God, I'm broken, I'm lost, I'm confused, but I know that you can take all things old and make them new in my life."

Satan wants to keep you from worshiping God, the One he hates. You will learn how to worship in season and out of season—when you're encouraged and discouraged. Our Enemy wants to keep you from doing the right thing. Whether that is spending time alone with God in prayer, meditating on his Word, attending and participating in public worship services, or any other thing that will draw you close to the Lord, he wants to distract you. He wants to discourage you. Your worship is the Enemy's discouragement. Your praise song is the sound of the devil's defeat!

You wandered in the wilderness, and the Enemy threw his best shot at you. He tried his best to deplete your faith, drain your joy, and dissolve your peace, but you know what? You're still here walking with God! You still have breath? You didn't pull the trigger? You didn't overdose? You didn't lose your mind in prison? The devil threw everything at you, and yet you're still married?

How is that possible?

Because you never stopped worshiping. You never stopped believing. Even when you worship discouraged, God's power will manifest in you and through you. Paul and Silas are the greatest example of that. The Bible says that before they were imprisoned, they were beaten almost to death. And yet what did they do? They chose to worship God despite their struggles. "Be thankful in all circumstances, for this is God's will for you who belong to Christ Jesus" (1 Thess. 5:18 NLT).

Maybe you feel like life has beaten you down to the point of death. Maybe you're going through a bitter divorce or you're facing a painful illness, and it feels like you don't know how you'll find the strength to keep going. Maybe someone left you, abandoned you, abused you, hurt you, discouraged you, let you down, left you disappointed. And now you're saying, "There's no more to life. I don't have purpose. I can't go on."

Paul and Silas were beaten down to the point of death, and then they were thrown into prison with chains and shackles. But the Bible says that one encouraged the other, and they began to worship God, with their baggage and with their chains, with their discouragement and with their disappointments, with their sin and with their neglect, with their dysfunction and with their brokenness. Nonetheless, they began to worship God, and they began to praise God, and they began to glorify God.

The devil made a stupid mistake. He had Paul and Silas flogged before throwing them in the inner cell and chaining their feet, but he did nothing about their mouths, the very thing that got them thrown in prison in the first place! I can just imagine the devil saying, *"No! Wait—how is this possible? They're barely alive, chained in jail, and they're* still *worshiping God?"* All the while, Paul and Silas just kept praying and worshiping, "God, I give you the glory. I give you the praise. You alone deserve all my worship." And guess what? The Bible says that while Paul and Silas were worshiping, a mighty earthquake came, broke their chains, and opened their prison doors (see Acts 16:16–40).

You can experience this same kind of liberation when faced with your own prisons in life. When you worship God in the midst of discouragement, your discouragement has to leave. In the presence of God, when you worship him in your pain, pain will be lifted. If you want to get through the wilderness to the more God has for you, then practice the power of worship. And remember, worship is a lifestyle, an everyday practice—not just an SOS when you're in trouble. When you make worship a part of your daily life, then you will naturally keep praising and worshiping God even when the ground shakes beneath your feet, whether literally or figuratively.

> *If you want to get through the wilderness to the more God has for you, then practice the power of worship.*

I-Witness Testimony

Finally, the last weapon against the Enemy is the power of your testimony. While traveling in Spain recently, I preached a sermon on the vital importance of sharing stories of your relationship with God, thereby creating a spiritual legacy for those around you. I compared this process to that of an athlete running a relay race, passing on the baton to the next runner, and learned that the Spanish word for baton is *testigo*, which literally means "testimony." I loved how perfectly this captured the whole point of having a testimony—to pass it on!

None of us runs the race of faith alone. You'll recall that

the passage I mentioned earlier from Hebrews 12 begins, "Since we are surrounded by such *a great cloud of witnesses,* let us throw off everything that hinders and the sin that so easily entangles" (Heb. 12:1, emphasis added). Think of all the believers who have gone before you, all the saints who endured persecution unto death and countless others. They're all cheering you on. They are witnesses who can provide testimony of God's saving grace in their lives.

Next time you're at a church service, look around you at the faces of the men and women in your congregation. Each one of them is a trophy testifying to God's power in their lives. Look on each face and see the stories etched in those little laugh lines and wrinkles around their eyes. There you will find their testimonies. Each have eyewitness accounts of how the Enemy tried to kill them but God saved them, how the devil tried to abuse them but God healed them, how Satan tried to discourage them but God lifted them up. And now they stand there, all different ages and backgrounds, radiating with the glory of God in their lives.

Some Sundays when I stand in the pulpit and look out, I get choked up looking into the faces of the people looking back at me and thinking about how their lives have been changed. I'm talking about people who were abusers and those who have been abused. I'm talking about gang members and those who were strung out on drugs and should have been dead, yet they're alive and walking in freedom and serving our church. They are living testimonies that God saved them, restored them, delivered them, and redeemed them.

Look around you at the witnesses.

And let others see what God has done in your own life.

Worship God for his grace. Worship him for his hand on your life. Watch and look around you, for there are witnesses who can testify of God's goodness. God has not brought you this far in life to abandon you in the wilderness. He has more for you, and you know it. So keep sharing the stories of what he has done already and what he is about to do. Speak the truth and let others hear it.

God has more for you. And now you have something to say. Say it. Speak it. Pass it on, for other people's chains can be broken because of how God delivered you. You've been there; you've done that. You've experienced Jesus, and you've experienced his power. Now pay it forward by blessing someone else.

Consider one more example from Paul's life. In Acts 27 we read about Paul surviving a terrible shipwreck. Left for dead, he wasn't supposed to survive this shipwreck, and somehow he found himself in a safe place. He landed on dry ground, grateful to feel it solid beneath his feet.

You would have thought that with everything Paul had been through up to that point, God might have showed some mercy and spared Paul going through another ordeal. However, God's thoughts are not our thoughts, our ways are not his ways (Isaiah 55:8). I believe that God chose not to spare Paul from this ordeal because there was something greater in store—there was something good God was working out for Paul. It might have looked really bad for Paul, but God's grace was sufficient. No matter what you're going through in your life, God's mercy will be on you, for there's a grace that is sufficient for you as well. You can do it because God would not set you up to fail you.

Paul and the other sailors landed on dry ground, and islanders came to help. The sailors and islanders didn't know each other, but the islanders were kind. God will set you up with helpful people as well. He will hook you up, for his plans never fail. The Bible says the islanders began to build a campfire because it was raining and cold. Paul gathered a pile of brush for the fire, and guess what happened? A viper, driven out by the heat of the fire, latched onto his hand. The natives standing around the fire were looking at Paul and saying, "That guy must be a murderer. He's gonna die for sure. He might have escaped dying in a shipwreck, but now the gods are gonna kill him on land."

See, people don't know the God you and I serve. They didn't recognize the God Paul served. And the viper came out of the fire and latched onto his hand—can you imagine? But rather than panic and be terrified by the doom and gloom the natives around him were proclaiming, Paul did something that you and I need to learn. "Paul shook the snake off into the fire and suffered no ill effects" (Acts 28:5).

Shake It Off

The Bible says Paul stood there with this snake attached to his hand, and he just shook it off. *He shook it off.* He didn't panic or try to run away. He didn't freak out or start feeling sorry for himself. He just shook it off.

How are you handling the vipers in your own life? Why are you letting them latch onto you, entertaining them, dressing them up, giving them a permanent home? Paul would not entertain the attack; when the attack came to him, he just shook it off. What do you need to shake off today so that you can experience the more God has for you?

You may be surprised at how quickly you can be back on your feet if you're willing to shake off those setbacks. I recall hearing a story about a donkey that fell into a deep pit in a remote village. Unable to get traction on the steep walls, the donkey grew tired and collapsed. The farmer who owned the poor donkey assumed the animal had died and began to shovel dirt into the pit to bury the beast. Each time the farmer shoveled in more dirt, the animal shook it off and stomped it into the ground beneath him, causing it to rise. Before long the donkey had risen several feet and then several more. Finally, he could escape, much to his owner's joy.

So shake off whatever gets thrown at you and get out of that pit! Shake off that depression. Shake off that fear. Shake off that doubt. Shake off that worry. The Bible says the viper came out of the fire. But Paul shook it off right back into the fire. When you shake off your troubles, right back into the fire they will go. Some of us need to remind the devil that out of the fire he comes, and right back to the fire he'll go.

Don't give the devil more than what he deserves. His future, his destiny, will be in the lake of fire, while you and I will be in heaven loving like Jesus and basking in the peace with which God has enveloped us.

God won't leave you in the wilderness.

The summer our church lost our auditorium and met in tents outdoors was one of the hardest times we endured. We had every kind of weather you can imagine that year—scorching temperatures, thunderstorms, even a hailstorm! The company that rented us our tent later told us that of the five tents they'd set up throughout Chicago, ours was the only one still standing at the end of the summer. Through every kind of weather, we persevered because we knew God had more for us. By that fall we discovered a property in the midst of our neighborhood for sale, an abandoned warehouse from the old Home Line Furniture Company.

I'm convinced we appreciated that property more because we understood what it meant to be homeless. We had been through the wilderness and could celebrate the promised land God had revealed to us.

God doesn't want you to be stagnant. He doesn't want you to give up hope just because you feel stuck. You have to move. You have to shake off those little vipers that jump out of the fire and latch onto you. You have to shake off shame, fear, discouragement, doubt, and worry.

> *You have to move. You have to shake off those little vipers that jump out of the fire and latch onto you.*

God has a special purpose for you. He has called you for more. The Enemy wants to distract you, but now you have some tools that you can use to distract him! You have the power of Jesus. You have the power of worship. And you have the power of your testimony. Walk with that. And when anything tries to come against you, speak with authority, for God is not going to leave you for dead. God will give you what you need. He has more for you just ahead.

PRAYING FOR MORE

Thank you, Jesus, for who you are. Thank you for your mercy. Thank you for your grace. I'm so grateful for the power and authority you give me to overcome the Enemy and his attempts to distract me. Help me stay focused on you no matter what my circumstances. No longer will I let disappointment and depression deter me from following you and discovering the more you have for me. You can do all things, Lord, because nothing is impossible for you. Thank you for all you're doing in my life, that which I can see and that which I will see in the future. I give you all the thanks and praise. Amen.

Chapter 6

DON'T MISS
YOUR MORE

No one can say yes to God's ways who has said no to
his promises and commandments. Acceptance of the will
of God comes in the daily submission under his Word.

—DIETRICH BONHOEFFER

W hat's the address again?" I asked. "There it is—up
ahead. Of course, it's on the opposite side of the street."
From the passenger seat, I pointed to my chiropractor's
office, in the middle of a busy block of shops and doctors'
offices. I was enjoying the luxury of having my assistant drive
me there so I wouldn't have to find a parking space, which in
downtown Chicago can take two minutes or twenty minutes.

The office was on the other side of the street, and my
assistant asked if he should make a U-turn or drive around
the block. I immediately told him not to make a U-turn but to
drive around the block instead. U-turns are illegal in our city,
so I took that opportunity to teach my young assistant a lesson.

As he drove around the block, I told him, "I know that a U-turn is a small thing and lots of people do them, and you probably would have gotten away with it. But it's important to pay attention to the small things. If you're getting away with this, what else are you allowing yourself to get away with?"

We were silent except for the swishing of the windshield wipers as he cruised around the side streets. I knew my assistant was just trying to be helpful. He had risen up through the youth team in our church, and I knew what a dedicated servant's heart he has for the Lord, for our ministry, and for me.

"If you start cutting corners with little things, then it makes it that much easier to give in when you're faced with a bigger temptation. Any time you compromise obedience, you risk losing the more God has for you."

"Well, I sure don't want to risk missing out on all God has for me because I made a U-turn!" he said, and we both laughed.

It Ain't Over Yet

Missing the more God has for you, however, is no laughing matter. Whenever I preach on discovering God's more in your life, usually a few people come up afterward and ask, "Pastor Choco, what do you do when you feel you've missed your more? I want to trust God at a deeper level with all areas of my life, but I've made so many mistakes, and now . . . well, I fear it's too late."

I'm always grateful when these brave individuals ask me this question, because I know there are many others who feel too embarrassed to ask. The fear of regret, of missing out on something big in one's life, is something most of us contend with. It may be during a crisis, and we're forced to wonder what would have happened if we had married a different person or chosen a different career path. Maybe we're facing an illness or injury, and we wish we had taken better care of our bodies and our health. It could be our finances and facing up to debt incurred in past years.

When you face these kinds of moments, they're only made worse when you realize that God has not been pleased with those past decisions. Suddenly you feel ashamed and afraid, insecure and uncertain. An emotional riptide is set off that tries to drag you under. What do you do when you have allowed fear to paralyze you, when you have allowed doubt to overcome you, when you have allowed selfish desires to dominate your life, when you have settled for less, and God is not pleased with your complacency? What do you do now?

You must know that missing your more doesn't mean you have lost all of what God has for you. It's not what you have lost but what you have left that counts. I like the idea that God is writing the story of my life. The Bible tells us to fix "our eyes on Jesus, the pioneer and perfecter of faith" (Heb. 12:2). He is authoring your story and mine. If we still have breath in us, he is not finished with our stories here on earth.

Regardless of what you have been through in your life, God is not done. No matter the mistakes you've made or the trials you've faced, you're just in a chapter. You

> *It's not what you have lost but what you have left that counts.*

may not like the particular chapter you're in right now, but God isn't finished. Imagine him saying, *"My child, I'm not done with you. I have other chapters for you. Your story is not finished."*

You may feel that your faith is weak and you're not strong enough. That's okay. But you must focus on Jesus, and he will finish what he started. God promises us this: "He who began a good work in you will carry it on to completion until the day of Christ Jesus" (Phil. 1:6). If you're struggling with missing your more, then this chapter is for you. I want to help you reclaim the more God has for you and save you from mistakes that might lead to missing out on all he has for you.

Civil Disobedience

How can you miss your more? The primary way is through partial obedience. When you're partially obeying, you're really not obeying at all. Delayed obedience is disobedience. There's no better example of this than the life of King Saul in the Old Testament. Most of the time Saul serves as an example of what *not* to do if you want to experience God's more.

Such is the case when God, through his prophet Samuel, told Saul, who had been chosen by God to be king over his people, to "attack the Amalekites and totally destroy all that belongs to them" (1 Sam. 15:3). Samuel relayed that God had been very specific about destroying everyone and everything—down to the last cow, goat, and sheep. We're told Saul gathered more than two-hundred thousand soldiers to wage war and annihilate this enemy tribe.

Somewhere along the way, Saul got creative with the instructions God had given him. He not only allowed Agag, the Amalekites' king, to live, but Saul also spared the best sheep and cattle and claimed them as spoils of his victory. We're told,

"Saul and the army spared . . . everything that was good. These they were unwilling to destroy completely, but everything that was despised and weak they totally destroyed" (1 Sam. 15:9).

God knew, of course, and immediately told Samuel, "I regret that I have made Saul king, because he has turned away from me and has not carried out my instructions" (v. 11). So Samuel went to see what in the world had happened. Saul greeted him with "The LORD bless you! I have carried out the LORD's instructions" (v. 13). Samuel basically replied, "Uh, did you, Saul? Did you really? Because what's the mooing and bleating I hear behind you there?" He may as well have said, "Liar, liar, pants on fire!" Samuel could see for himself how Saul had disobeyed and knew why God was so upset with the man he had chosen to lead his people.

Then it got worse.

Saul said, "But I did obey! It was the soldiers—they were the ones who decided to keep the best cows and sheep. They did it!" Where I come from, we call that throwing them under the bus; although, maybe in Saul's time it was more like throwing them under the chariot. Isn't human nature interesting when we get caught? Whether it's Adam and Eve in the garden blaming the serpent or your kids pointing fingers at each other, human tendency is to shift blame and find someone to be the scapegoat. My kids used to say, "Don't look at me! I didn't do it! It was [fill in the blank with their siblings in closest proximity]—they're the ones who did it." Saul even tried to explain why the soldiers kept the best animals; he claimed they kept the fattest calves and purest sheep to sacrifice to God.

But Samuel didn't buy it. He told Saul, "Does the LORD delight in burnt offerings and sacrifices as much as in obeying the LORD? To obey is better than sacrifice, and to heed is better than the fat of rams" (v. 22). Busted! At this point Saul knew he'd blown it and began to beg for forgiveness and a second chance. He asked Samuel to go worship with him, to make things right between Saul and God. But it was too late. Samuel told him, "I will not go back with you. You have rejected the word of the LORD, and the LORD has rejected you as king over Israel!" (v. 26).

Samuel turned to leave, but Saul kept begging and even grabbed the prophet's robe, tearing off a piece. Samuel made it clear that this was all Saul had left—a remnant of the role God had initially given him. Instead of wearing the royal cloak of a king, Saul stood holding the tattered hem of someone else's garment. He had partially obeyed, which is to say he had disobeyed, and missed the more that God had for him.

No Excuses

Partial obedience is still disobedience. Just imagine you sent your child to go clean their room, but when you returned an hour later you noticed that it was only partially done. They made their bed, but they left their dirty clothes lying on the floor. Some toys were picked up, but others cluttered their desk along with books and papers.

"Why didn't you clean your room?" you ask.

"But I did clean my room! I made my bed, see?" your child says.

"No, you started cleaning your room, but you haven't finished. Cleaning your room means all of it, not just what you decide you feel like doing."

Sometimes our children seem to think that we should celebrate the fact they picked up their socks or made their bed when everything else around them remains to be done. Would you say they obeyed your request without cleaning their entire room? I don't think most of us would.

Or consider a half-done construction job at your house. You asked for a complete kitchen renovation, but when you come in, only part of it is done. There's tile on part

Partial obedience is still disobedience.

of the floor but not all of it. Some cabinets have been replaced but not all. You have a new fridge but the same old stove that doesn't work. The job is unfinished and incomplete.

Nevertheless, the contractor says, "I'm done—pay up. I came in on budget for the amount estimated."

And you protest, saying, "Wait a minute! You didn't even finish."

"So what?" he replies. "You should be satisfied with what I started."

It doesn't make sense. There's no way you or I would be satisfied with a half-done job like this. But apparently Saul expected God to find a half-done job acceptable. The king thought he could do his own thing.

Let me say it again: partial obedience is disobedience.

And there's nothing for you and me to celebrate when we partially obey God. "But I did obey the Lord," Saul said. "I went on the mission the Lord assigned me, and I completely destroyed the Amalekites and brought back Agag as a prisoner of war. I killed all the livestock except for the very best, which we planned to offer as a sacrifice."

Who did he think he was kidding? Saul sounded worse

than a Chicago politician when it's time for reelection! He was contradicting himself. "I did destroy them all. Well, except for their king. I did kill all the living creatures—except for the best ones, which we'll sacrifice." But then Samuel clarified a major problem with Saul's definition of obedience: "Does the LORD delight in burnt offerings and sacrifices as much as in obeying the LORD? To obey is better than sacrifice, and to heed is better than the fat of rams" (1 Sam. 15:22).

To obey is better than sacrifice.

Partial obedience is based on the assumption that you're the exception to the rule. It's thinking, *Well, sure, everyone else needs to obey, but I'm special. I'm obeying God—I'm just doing it in my own way, the way I want to do it.* Partial obedience seeks self-recognition. When I partially obey, I seek to be acknowledged. Someone who suffers from low self-esteem or insecurity always wants to be recognized. As you interact with the people around you, notice the person who says, "Wow, you won't believe what I did last weekend!" or "You should come see what we just bought for our deck," or "I don't want to drop names, but you'll never guess who I just had lunch with!" When they start talking like that—"I did this and I bought that and I know so-and-so"—there's a good chance they struggle with self-esteem issues. People who have insecurities have to build trophies. Saul's prisoner of war, King Agag, was a trophy. Saul basically said, "Look what I did! I won! I killed all these people, and here's my trophy, their king." Because Saul suffered from insecurity, he had to have a trophy—even at the expense of disobeying God. As a matter of fact, if you continue to read his story in Scripture, you'll see that Saul built a monument in his own honor (1 Sam. 15:12).

Now there's nothing wrong with winning trophies. We've probably all won some academic award or some trophy from playing sports in school. Even I have trophies from those past glory days on the baseball team in Humboldt Park. But I'm not at home admiring and polishing them every day. Who has time for that? I surely don't, and I'm guessing you don't either. Trophies are fine, but some people worship them, always wanting to be recognized for what they did. People like King Saul suffer from insecurity and from low self-esteem, and this struggle can be dangerous. When you start looking at your trophies and accomplishments, and you admire them, and you want someone else to admire them, you're creating an idol for yourself and discrediting God. When Saul chose to take a trophy rather than fully obeying God, he lost the blessing God had for him.

He lost his more.

Spoiling the Vine

Another way to miss your more is by not taking care of the details, what the Song of Songs refers to as "the little foxes that ruin the vines" (2:15). These are the little things in your life that can prevent you from growing and maturing to your full potential. They don't seem like big deals at the time—much like my assistant wanting to make a U-turn to drop me off.

You think, *I'm in a hurry to get home and be with my family, so it's okay if I speed. Or I can take these pens and that box of printer paper home from the office—there's so much no one will miss it. I'm always working at home anyway.* We disobey in some small way and then justify it as inconsequential. But over time these little instances of cutting corners create a pattern of compromise.

If you do not take care of these small habits in your life at twenty, at thirty, at forty, they eat away at your productivity and growth, which are the fruit you have to show for your life. Solomon, the wisest man who ever lived, addressed this problem in Scripture by admonishing: "Catch us the foxes, the little foxes that spoil the vines, for our vines have tender grapes" (Song 2:15 NKJV).

You know what foxes do? Foxes don't come after the fruit in the vineyard—they go after the vine, the lifeline for the tender grapes. Jesus said, "I am the vine; you are the branches" (John 15:5). When we allow little things to slide and don't follow the rules, we open the gate and let these little foxes into our lives. The devil doesn't care about your fruit! He wants to sever your relationship to the vine, to Christ. He is after that which is feeding you in your pursuit of being the man or woman God created you to be.

And you must keep in mind that whatever you don't confront today, your kids will have to face tomorrow. Whatever you allow to destroy the vine in your life as a young person, if you don't have the courage to kill these pesky foxes in your life, they're going to grow. If you're married and have children, your children will face them and have to kill them because you didn't have the courage to eliminate them. This insecurity, this jealousy that you have, this lack of confidence, this self-esteem issue, this tendency to exaggerate and lie, to borrow permanently, to gossip—they all must be destroyed. The devil will use these things, and he will kill the vine that's feeding your life.

Saul let these foxes run loose in his life, and it destroyed him. During the tense exchange that Samuel had with Saul after the battle, the prophet told the king, "Although you were once small in your own eyes, did you not become the head of the tribes of Israel? The LORD anointed you king over Israel" (1 Sam. 15:17). Saul's struggle with insecurity was no secret, and Samuel reminded him of it. But he also reminded Saul of a major change that should have clobbered this inferiority complex once and for all: *God chose him to be king*!

Insecurity will cause you to partially obey, to do things halfheartedly, and to settle for mediocrity. When we place our identity and self-worth in our accomplishments instead of who God says we are and how he values us, we set ourselves up to miss our more. If you want to experience God's more, you must build on what God sees, not on what you see.

> *And you must keep in mind that whatever you don't confront today, your kids will have to face tomorrow.*

Numerous articles by psychologists and therapists, including one I recently read in *Psychology Today*, reinforce the truth that insecure people need to showcase their accomplishments. In her article "The Epidemic of Insecurity," Beverly D. Flaxington points out the way social media reinforces and compounds this human tendency. Social media not only encourages us to document every moment of every day but to present it in the best possible light. When we're online and see how amazing everyone else's lives look, we feel even more insecure. This insecurity tempts us to post our own trophies of status, wealth, and accomplishment.

Flaxington cites a recent university study in Sweden that examined the relationship between Facebook usage and users' levels of self-assurance: "The researchers found that prolonged Facebook usage negatively impacted the users' self-esteem, with women being more affected than men. Considering the fact that there are over 1.39 billion monthly active Facebook users globally, the findings of the study reflect a truly alarming tendency."[2]

While King Saul didn't have to contend with comparisons on Facebook and critical trolls online, he still suffered from "looking small in his own eyes." As a result of his personal weakness, he chose to pursue looking good in the eyes of his people instead of the eyes of the Lord. Not only did he not fully obey by destroying the Amalekites and everything that belonged to them, but he chose not to wait for the prophet to come to offer a sacrifice. Maybe this doesn't seem like a big deal to us today, especially when we're considering a guy who was a king. But performing this kind of sacrifice was a sacred rite performed only by priests and prophets, God's holy men.

This wasn't the first time public opinion caused Saul to act impulsively and seek people's approval instead of God's. The seeds for Saul's narcissism had been planted back when he was first inaugurated as king. Samuel had explained the duties and responsibilities of a king and introduced Saul as God's chosen and anointed sovereign for Israel, but not everyone was on board with their new leader. The majority of the crowd may have cheered their new king, "but some scoundrels said, 'How can this fellow save us?' They despised him and brought him no gifts. But Saul kept silent" (1 Sam. 10:27).

It was customary for people to bring gifts to their new monarch, much like we see later at the birth of Jesus when the magi traveling from the East present him with gold, frankincense, and myrrh. At Saul's big moment, he had some hecklers who refused to respect him in this traditional manner. While Scripture indicates that Saul kept silent, I'm betting he didn't forget something like that. Many people who suffer from low self-esteem fixate on the one negative comment they get instead of on the hundreds of positive affirmations.

This incident serves as a good reminder that whatever offense you and I experience and remain silent about will only get worse if we don't handle it. Obviously, Saul felt slighted and disrespected by these critics in his coronation crowd. And yet he kept silent. He allowed that seed of rejection to grow in his heart and silently fester and grow into a cancer poisoning him with fear, envy, and the need to please people.

Fox Hunt

How do you stop those little foxes? There's a sure-fire trap that extinguishes them every time: repentance. When we repent, we chase out the little foxes that have been roaming inside us, nibbling away at the vines of faith in our hearts. We clear the slate and ask God to forgive us and to restore us in our relationships with him. We start over and once again open the way to receive all that God wants to give us and to do in our lives.

Repentance begins with confession, an admission of the sinful way we have strayed away from God and his assignment for our lives. Confession restores our health like a brisk tonic on our skin. It's refreshing to say to your loved one or your family, to your kids or your friends, "Hey, I did wrong; my bad. I'm sorry." You aren't diminished as a man or woman of God when you repent. Instead, repentance shows your humility and your reliance on God as the source of your identity and self-worth. Next, we must thank God for the forgiveness that he has given us. Thank God for his forgiveness, that he has forgiven us a thousand times, and that he chooses not to remember your sins or my sins anymore.

So, we must admit, we must thank God for the forgiveness, and finally, we must commit to the new assignment.

If we wish to fully repent and eliminate those little ways we compromise our full obedience, then we must commit to the assignment that God has given us. We must say, "Hey, starting today, right now, I'm making this new commitment. I can't allow these little foxes in my life that are destroying me, these bad habits, these bad attitudes, this condescending spirit. I can't have it." You must commit yourself to the assignment that God has for you, because if you do not, you're going to miss your more. You're going to miss what God has.

The king who followed Saul offered a sharp contrast in the area of repentance. In many ways, David made just as many mistakes as his predecessor—he too disobeyed God and went his own way at times. You might recall his relationship with a certain bathing beauty named Bathsheba. The striking difference between Saul and David is what each man did after he messed up. Saul justified his sin, shifted blame, and withdrew. And while David may have done similar things, he ultimately returned to God, wrecked and broken by his rebellious, sinful heart.

David repented and made sure he didn't miss the more God had for him. He wrote one of my favorite prayers of repentance, one that's guaranteed to give you a fox-proof faith:

Create in me a pure heart, O God,
    and renew a steadfast spirit within me.
Do not cast me from your presence
    or take your Holy Spirit from me.
Restore to me the joy of your salvation
    and grant me a willing spirit, to sustain me.
    (Ps. 51:10–12)

Never Settle for Less

When you miss your more, it's often because you have settled. You have settled yourself in a place and stopped before reaching the destination God had for you. When Terah, the father of Abraham, left his homeland with his sons and their families, he went in search of the new place God wanted them to call home, which was Canaan, the promised land. But Terah got tired, and he ended up settling in the city of Harran (Gen. 11:31–32). Basically, Terah said, "I'm done. I know I'm supposed to go to Canaan, but I'm going to settle here at Harran instead." He chose his own comfort and convenience rather than obeying God for something more.

You probably know people who settle for less. They're the ones who give up and say, "I can't do it anymore." They resign themselves to stopping where they are and not trying to go any further.

> *When you miss your more, it's often because you have settled.*

They accept that this is the way things are going to be, that this is their life. And for the rest of their life, they're always complaining. They were never supposed to settle in Harran.

Why settle for a lesser land when God has offered the promised land?

And what about you, my friend? You might not like this, but I must ask: Where have you settled for less than God's more in your life? In your career? Your family? In your willingness to lead? In your relationships?

We have so many teens and young adults in our church that I see settling and dating someone—often a nonbeliever—who is not the partner God has for them. Their lifestyles contradict one another and their values pull in opposite directions, but these single guys and gals don't want to be alone. They're so desperate for someone to love them and make them feel special and important that they take whoever is available.

When I've tried to talk to them, some have even said, "It's no big deal. We're just friends. It's not going anywhere."

I tell them, "Well, if it's not going anywhere, then get out of there! You don't need them right now. God loves you and says you have value as his precious child. Don't settle for less!" God makes it clear in his Word that we are not to be yoked with nonbelievers. It's just too hard to be united in marriage with someone who doesn't share the same core beliefs that impact every area of a believer's life.

You know what happens when you settle? You die—just like Terah died in Harran. When he gave up reaching Canaan, I wonder if he lost his will to live—he settled, and then he died. Whatever you do, don't settle. Keep moving forward, even if you have to drag yourself, step-by-step and day by day. Even if you're tired and weary and hurting and bleeding, keep moving forward. Experiencing God's more is about moving forward—making progress, not settling for less.

Don't miss your more. Don't be like Saul and try to pick and choose when and how you obey God. Remain faithful in all things, and obey God fully, not just partially. Get rid of those little foxes in your life, those habits and compromises that you justify as harmless. Realize the cumulative impact they can have on you, your life, and your legacy. If you don't want to miss God's more in your life, then repent and turn back to God. Don't settle for second best. Follow God to your promised land!

PRAYING FOR MORE

Lord, sometimes I feel like I've missed my more. I feel like I've settled. I've allowed those little foxes in my life that are destroying the vine, my relationship with you, the nourishment to my life. Help me get rid of these foxes and to secure the garden of my heart for you, Jesus, and you alone. Forgive me for sliding in my faith and settling for less. I'm sorry that I forget who you say I am and then run to my friends or rush to get online so others will validate me. I know that my life is only significant because you made me and love me. God, I repent of the many ways I've failed, and I thank you for the mercy, grace, and pardon you freely give. Wash me and make me clean so that I may receive the more you have for me. Amen.

Chapter 7

WHEN LESS IS MORE

The greatest legacy one can pass on to one's children and grandchildren is not money or other material things accumulated in one's life, but rather a legacy of character and faith.

—BILLY GRAHAM

When I think about the life I envisioned for myself when Elizabeth and I first married more than two decades ago, I just have to shake my head and smile. We're not where I thought we'd be. As a *jovencito* coming out of a gang-infested, crime-ridden area of Chicago, I was determined, with the Lord's help, to make a better life for myself and my family. I didn't want to be extravagantly wealthy, but when I was a kid, being rich simply meant living in a safe home, paying bills on time, and having plenty of food in the pantry. And I did want that kind of life, a better life, for Elizabeth and me.

Growing up was a stressful adventure. Because my mother couldn't keep up on rent, we often stayed with aunts and uncles until we could afford a new place. My older brother was in a gang, and I often came home from school and was told that my mom had gone to see him in the hospital or to pick him up at the police station. Scraping by and relying on food stamps and government assistance was a way of life, one that many in our community accepted or even embraced. But I despised it.

I wanted more for my life than to belong to a gang and escape through drugs and alcohol, and so I vowed never to live like my parents. And since I wasn't the greatest student—I failed third grade—I knew the only way I could have this better life was through hard work. I was committed to doing whatever it took to escape Humboldt Park.

Once I became a Christian, my desire for a stable, more secure future didn't change. But I also began to see God provide for my needs and surprise me with an abundance of blessings I never expected. From reading his Word, I knew God wanted my best efforts: "Whatever you do, work at it with all your heart, as working for the Lord, not for human masters" (Col. 3:23). So I worked hard and planned on providing for my family so that we could have more than I had growing up.

The last thing I wanted to do was become a pastor. Working a variety of jobs, I had my sights set on law enforcement or possibly sales. Elizabeth was the daughter of a pastor and knew firsthand that it wasn't an easy life. She, like me, hoped our family would have just a little bit more than she had growing up.

If you had asked either of us on our wedding day what having more meant, the answer would have been living in a nice home in a good neighborhood, driving a car (all panels the same color) that consistently started, and maybe taking a vacation every few years. We didn't want to get pulled in by our culture's emphasis on money, possessions, and consumerism, but we also wanted more than either of us had growing up.

What we've discovered over the years is that our human views of more and God's definition don't always align. Even if we're not caught up in driving a new luxury car, wearing designer clothes, and eating in trendy restaurants, we still might not understand God's definition. We often find God's more in the midst of what we lose, as well as in the losses of others. This is the paradox of God's more. We lose our lives for his sake to find true joy, peace, and fulfillment. Just when you thought you lost your more, you discover God had something much greater in mind for you.

> *We often find God's more in the midst of what we lose.*

Embracing the Storms

In chapter 2 I shared with you why Paul remains one of my personal heroes of the faith. The dramatic encounter he had with God transformed him from Saul, the murderous persecutor of Christ-followers, into Paul, the fearless global preacher of the gospel. This powerful change is reason enough to admire him, but it's not why I return to Paul's life and writings again and again. The reason I love Paul so much is because he learned that to experience God's more, we must focus less on ourselves. Life wasn't about what was in it for him but what was in it for the kingdom. Because he was marked for more and called to more by God, Paul experienced contentment no matter what the circumstances of his life might be.

Writing to the community of Christians in Philippi, Paul

concluded his letter by thanking the believers there for supporting him and his ministry, presumably with gifts of money, food, and supplies. But right after expressing his gratitude, he also made it clear that he was fine whether they were able to support him or not:

> I am not saying this because I am in need, for I have learned to be content whatever the circumstances. I know what it is to be in need, and I know what it is to have plenty. I have learned the secret of being content in any and every situation, whether well fed or hungry, whether living in plenty or in want. I can do all this through him who gives me strength. (Phil. 4:11–13)

The guy writing this is the same man who endured shipwrecks, beatings, imprisonment, earthquakes, and persecution for the sake of the gospel. We don't know whether Paul had a cushy life before he met Jesus on the road to Damascus, but we do know he definitely didn't have one afterward. When you study Paul's life, you discover he was the type of guy who didn't question God when things went wrong. He embraced the storms. He didn't doubt his faith when events didn't turn out the way he wanted them to turn out. He always had a greater perspective of his life and his circumstances. He always knew that God was in control. He never lost heart.

Paul addressed people in all spectrums of life and tried to reach them right where they were. He could relate to wealthy leaders and to imprisoned slaves, to Gentiles as well as Jews, women as well as men. He wrote, "Though I am free and belong to no one, I have made myself a slave to everyone, to win as many as possible. . . . I have become all things to all people so that by all possible means I might save some" (1 Cor. 9:19, 22).

I remind myself along with those in our church to remember Paul's humility and willingness to relate to others, regardless of their differences. In our present polarized culture, we would all do well to follow Paul's example. Our differences shouldn't prevent us from respecting, relating, and reaching out to one another. Paul made this very clear: "There is neither Jew nor Gentile, neither slave nor free, nor is there male and female, for you are all one in Christ Jesus" (Gal. 3:28).

Even though he could relate with everyone, Paul never compromised his convictions about God's truth and the power of the gospel. Paul was sold out to God and loved people enough not to pull any punches. He was tired of the religion thing because he had already done that in his old life as Saul, and it only led to legalism and a performance-based faith that felt impossible to fulfill.

When he spoke, when he evangelized—whether in person or in his letters—he communicated with great passion, conviction, and sincerity. And Paul never told people what they necessarily wanted to hear; he told them what they *needed* to hear—reminding them of both their sinfulness as well as God's grace and mercy.

Thorn in My Flesh

Because of his frequent travels, Paul often wrote letters, also called epistles, to various churches he had visited or helped start. These were later collected in our New Testament. In one of these letters to the church at Corinth, Paul directly addressed the paradox of experiencing God's more when we let go of our attempts to have more.

> Even if I should choose to boast, I would not be a fool, because I would be speaking the truth. But I refrain, so no one will think more of me than is warranted by what I do or say, or because of these surpassingly great revelations. Therefore, in order to keep me from becoming conceited, I was given a thorn in my flesh, a messenger of Satan, to torment me. Three times I pleaded with the Lord to take it away from me. But he said to me, "My grace is sufficient for you, for my power is made perfect in weakness." Therefore I will boast all the more gladly about my weaknesses, so that Christ's power may rest on me. That is why, for Christ's sake, I delight in weaknesses, in insults, in hardships, in persecutions, in difficulties. For when I am weak, then I am strong. (2 Cor. 12:6–10)

Let's look at the context of this passage before we explore it. In an earlier letter Paul had written, he told the Corinthians that he would be joining them soon (1 Cor. 16). Time passed— we're not told exactly how long, but enough time that people started to worry and to gossip. The people in Corinth began to question the facts of their faith, even wondering if Paul was really a true apostle.

Many of them knew Jesus had only twelve disciples during his time on earth, and Paul had not been one of them. The original Twelve, with the exception of Judas who betrayed his Lord and then hanged himself afterward, had all been eyewitnesses to Jesus's life, miracles, death on the cross, and resurrection. They were eyewitnesses and participants in the earthly ministry of the Messiah. They had street cred that Paul lacked. If Paul didn't have this firsthand experience to draw on, then how could he be so sure the gospel was true?

So Paul wrote 2 Corinthians to the believers in Corinth, giving them instructions and reminding them of his personal encounter with God and subsequent calling, despite the fact that he was not one of the original Twelve. He wanted to let them know, "Hey, I might not be there physically, but it's not me that you need to focus on. It's the Lord above that I want you to keep your eyes on. Even if I didn't meet Jesus in the flesh, I ran into him head-on in the spirit! The gospel I preached to you is true because it is from the Lord."

Paul also knew that a lot of sexual immorality was happening within the church and that many false teachers were rising up in the community. So Paul wrote to encourage the church at this time not to forfeit their faith, not to give up on what they believed. Being the kind of relatable, humble guy who liked to come alongside others, Paul wanted to make it clear that he too had struggles in his life. He didn't specify what he struggled with, but he described it as a "thorn in my flesh" and a "messenger of Satan" (2 Cor. 12:7). That sounds like a pretty tough battle to me!

Paul knew he was allowed to struggle with this thorn to keep him from becoming conceited (2 Cor. 12:7). Nevertheless, Paul still prayed for God to deliver him from this problem three times, and the answer was the same each time: "My grace is sufficient for you, for my power is made perfect in weakness" (2 Cor. 12:9). Instead of being disappointed like you or I might be, Paul rejoiced in God's reply because he knew it meant he would be forced to continue depending on the Lord.

Paul couldn't remove this thorn and overcome its pain, and God didn't remove it for him. It was something Paul had to live with, to face daily, to push through, to battle in the midst of his ministry and the other circumstances of his life. And what he discovered still holds true for us today: *"When I am weak, then I am strong"* (2 Cor. 12:10, emphasis added).

Where Credit Is Due

Looking back at all Paul accomplished and how the Holy Spirit inspired him to write these letters that are part of God's Word, we realize that Paul had plenty to boast about. But he chose not to boast in the things he had earned, the churches he had started, and the sermons he had preached. Deep down inside, he knew he could not have done any of these things by himself. He understood that he needed help. Paul was not willing to take the glory and praise for these accomplishments because he knew they really didn't belong to him. So he took the spotlight and pointed it right back to God.

If you think this isn't a big deal, I promise you it is. Any type of pulpit ministry, stage ministry, or worship or performance ministry plays to our human pride. I've struggled with it. Whenever I preach or speak at a conference, I'm tempted to accept all the compliments and praise for myself. I can remember how amazing I felt after my first few sermons. I'd be greeting people in the aisle or standing back by the door to shake hands as they left. Many of them would say, "Pastor, that was a great word you just gave us from the Lord!" or "Great sermon today, Pastor Choco—you spoke right to me."

It was hard for me to believe these encouraging comments because I never thought of myself as a great public speaker and certainly not as a biblical scholar or preacher. Like I said, I failed third grade, and I ended up skipping eighth grade altogether!

You see, when I was in seventh grade near the end of the school year, there was a fire in our apartment building. Mom had to move us to temporary housing until we could find something permanent. Because we moved to a different part of the city, I had to switch schools to finish the year, and some kind of mix-up occurred. My old school must have indicated I was going into eighth grade, and my new school assumed that this meant I was finishing it.

Next thing I knew, I was sitting up on stage with a bunch of eighth graders at my new school in a middle school graduation ceremony! I remember my mom being there and acting so proud and getting tears in her eyes as I sat there thinking, *This is crazy! What happened? Any moment now someone is going to walk in and yell, "Wait a minute—there's been a mistake!"* But no one ever came. The really funny part, and one that may even have been a little prophetic, was the class song, "The Impossible Dream." I sang that song as loud as I could. And I smile now when I think of myself sitting there with my new friends, wondering how long that dream would last, waiting for someone to figure it out and take it all away.

Years later I was asked to be the keynote speaker for a graduation in that same school, and even then I thought someone was going to figure it out. Standing on that same stage, I was a little afraid the principal was going to ask for my eighth-grade diploma back! But he didn't. Looking back, I like to think that God was giving me back that year when I repeated third grade.

I tell you this so you can realize how incredible it was when people started thanking me and complimenting me on my teaching and speaking. The funny thing is that I know better. I know there's no way I can do anything on my own and take the credit for it. In the past few years, other pastors have asked me, "Choco, what's your master plan? How have you decided where to start the next campus? What variables do you factor in when starting a new church ministry?"

Again, I just have to shake my head and laugh because there is no master plan! Other campuses under the umbrella of our church have started when a group has started meeting and growing, when someone like Pastor John Hannah has a burden for the people of Chicago and receives a calling from God to partner with us. That's how our church has grown—and that's the only way. By listening for God's voice and following him every step of the way.

You can ask Elizabeth or my kids or some of my team members, and they'll tell you that most days I'm just making it happen! In my circle, "make it happen" is understood as putting your hand to the plow and trusting what God said in the first place when things seem a little uncertain, a little complicated, or even intimidating. Yes, I prepare and work hard and do my homework, but what keeps me going is knowing my limitations and weaknesses and relying on God's power and the Spirit's leading. I know that my more will never satisfy or have an impact on others the way God's more will.

> *In my circle, "make it happen" is understood as putting your hand to the plow and trusting what God said in the first place.*

Security Systems

The harder you work within your own power to have more, the more you will be tempted to seek the applause of others. This is what many people believe happened to Satan. As the angel Lucifer, he was in charge of music and worship in heaven (Ezek. 28:13; Isa. 14:12–15). Then he started wondering why he wasn't the star of the show instead of God. I can just imagine him saying, *"How is it that I'm leading worship and not getting any credit? They're praising, yet God's getting all the glory! Maybe it's time for me to claim the glory for myself."*

You're in a dangerous position when all you want to do is receive more and more without giving the rightful credit to your Source. Paul avoided this trap by having his weakness right in front of him every day. As much as it pained him, the thorn in his flesh reminded him that he could never take credit for anything. Anytime Paul received credit, he gave it back to God.

We must do the same. And we must be careful with people who like to boast about their accomplishments and sing their own praises. Be careful with people who like to post all their awards and prizes on their status page so everyone can see how great they are. Be wary of people who are always showing off their latest purchase or prized possession. They may not even realize what they're doing, but clearly they want attention. They want to be envied and adored, admired and emulated.

When we feed into their egos, we're ultimately feeding into their insecurity. You may not mean to feed into their struggles with low self-esteem or with arrogance, but that's what you're doing when you text them a compliment, give them a retweet, or tell them how much you love their latest posting.

Truth be told, we all struggle with insecurity. Maybe others in your life don't struggle as much with this kind of insecurity as you do. Are you constantly checking your Facebook page and seeing how many likes you have? Does your YouTube channel have more subscribers than your best friend's? How many people are following your tweets? If your self-worth is linked to social media or anything other than God's truth, then you're likely too preoccupied to experience God's more.

We can't focus on people's accomplishments more than on the people themselves. Don't focus more on their medals and résumés than on what's going on in their hearts. Don't assume your friends have their lives together because of their smiling vacation pics posted on Instagram. Don't envy your cousin's promotion without knowing how she struggles in her marriage.

Many times as parents we look at our children and push them toward collecting trophies, trying to live our past dreams, rather than seeing them for who they are and what their hearts contain. We push them without even really knowing them. We think this is what they want. We assume they're doing it because they enjoy it, but they really just want to spend time with us and have our approval.

We can't live our dreams through our children or other people, fantasizing about having their careers, thinking that a snapshot of their HGTV-styled kitchen or their latest party pics on social media accurately represent their lives. We don't realize that behind closed doors most people are fighting for their lives. They're panicked about how much debt they're in. They're heartsick over the choices their kids are making. They're terrified that their spouse is going to leave them.

They're just looking for approval. They're looking for

something that can make them feel good about themselves. They're looking for your likes. They're looking for your words of affirmation. They're looking for your counsel. The problem with all of this is that your counsel, your likes, your approvals eventually die out. This explains why it's important for us not to feed into their ego or into their insecurity but to point them to the One who can give them an everlasting sense of worth, peace, and purpose.

You and I are limited in what we can give others.

But with God, there's no ceiling.

What Money Can't Buy

Pride attempts to provide security for the very things missing in our lives. Because we feel unfulfilled, we look for attention from others about our awards, purchases, and experiences. We feel deprived of the love we long for inside, so we look to get it from a romantic relationship or sexual encounter. We lack the security of knowing who we really are as God's children and instead place our identity in our jobs, in our salaries, in our association with celebrities.

When we allow our pride to poison our hearts, we end up living conditionally. We think that once we attain our dreams or find the longings of our hearts, we'll be whole. We think, *If I can have children, then I'll be happy for the rest of my life. If I can make all the money in the world, then I can be happy for the rest of my life. If I can gain my dream car or my dream house, I'll finally be content.*

But chasing after possessions and personal dreams only

leaves us empty. We become so preoccupied and self-absorbed that we no longer hear God's voice or allow the Spirit to guide us. We cling so tightly to our lives and all the stuff we try to cram into them that there is no room for God and all he wants to give us.

It's an old struggle. A wealthy young man approached Jesus and asked him, "What is it that I need to do to gain eternal life? What is it that I should do?" (see Matt. 19:16–22).

Think about it. He was a rich man; he was successful; he had everything. But he was looking for something money can't buy. Jesus simply told him, "I want you to obey the commandments." And then Jesus went right down the list of commandments.

The rich man said, "I've kept all of these. What else do I lack?"

He had everything, yet he still felt as though he were lacking something. Obviously he wasn't lacking in any material possessions. He had lots of money, more than enough to buy anything he wanted.

Jesus told him, "If you want to be perfect and complete, then go and sell all your possessions, and give the money to the poor, and you will have treasures in heaven. Then come, follow me."

I suspect the rich man must have had an "aha" moment right then. Or maybe it was closer to an "oh no!" moment. A moment when he thought, *Jesus, are you serious? You're telling me I've got to get rid of all my stuff in order to follow you and have eternal life?* It was a condition he was unwilling to meet. We're told the rich young man went away very sad (Matt. 19:22).

Jesus then turned to his disciples and said, "Truly I tell you, it is hard for someone who is rich to enter the kingdom of heaven" (Matt. 19:23). I wonder if Jesus was thinking, *What a shame it is that you're willing to keep temporary security in your possessions, in your pride. It brings some comfort to you, yet you forfeit your security in eternity all because you aren't willing to lose what you have so I can give you what you long for.*

Losing to Win

Jesus's response to this rich young dude was not the only time he warned us about the temptations to put our treasure in earthly possessions instead of his eternal kingdom. He knew human beings tend to want a concrete, tangible kind of more instead of just the invisible, eternal, spiritual kind. While God often showers us with an abundance of material blessings, they are not what his more is all about. Jesus made it clear that wealth isn't the problem—it's what goes on in our hearts when we view money as our god instead of utilizing it as a resource from the living God. As part of Christ's Sermon on the Mount (Matt. 5–7), he told us,

> Do not store up for yourselves treasures on earth, where moths and vermin destroy, and where thieves break in and steal. But store up for yourselves treasures in heaven, where moths and vermin do not destroy, and where thieves do not break in and steal. For where your treasure is, there your heart will be also. . . .
>
> No one can serve two masters. Either you will hate the one and love the other, or you will be devoted to the one and despise the other. You cannot serve both God and money. (Matt. 6:19–21, 24)

Wealthy people like the rich young ruler are not the only ones who struggle with this dilemma of putting their faith and trust in God or in money. Growing up poor, I understandably viewed money as the answer to most problems. As a kid I'd think, *If only my mom earned more money, we could live in a better place and not have to move all the time. If only we had money, we could pay the bills on time and get whatever we want to eat at the store. If only we had money, I could go to college and get a good job.* Although we didn't have much money, I was still giving money as much power in my life as someone who was rich.

But what I learned after becoming a Christian is that money has no power in and of itself—as a resource, it only has the limited power we assign to it. Only God has real power, the kind of power that can heal the sick and feed the five thousand, the kind of power that can defeat death once and for all, the kind of power that can forgive our sins and satisfy our hearts. When we attempt to find our hope, security, and power in money, we will eventually end up disappointed. And when we waste our time idolizing wealth, we miss out on the true spiritual riches God has for us.

As painful as it may feel at the time, losing is sometimes the best thing that can happen to us. Do you ever think back in your life and feel so grateful that the person you used to be with, that joker you used to live with, or that individual you used to call your boyfriend or your girlfriend is now no longer part of your life? Instead, you say, "Thank you, Jesus, that they are no longer a part of my life! The loss was hard at that moment, but today I'm grateful. You had so much more for me that I just couldn't see at the time."

Sometimes losing is winning—you just don't realize it.

Have you ever lost something that later made you stronger? Maybe you have lost some friends, some influential people in your life. They influenced you to think wrong, do wrong. They influenced you to talk wrong, walk wrong. Now you have disconnected yourself from that, and you say, "Thank you, Jesus. I loved them, but I can no longer be connected to them. I thought I needed them to feel okay, but you wanted to give me more."

Maybe you have things in your life right now that you need to let go of, things that you use to define you, to give you security, or to provide a sense of worth.

> *Sometimes losing is winning—you just don't realize it.*

Maybe you're struggling with your own thorn. You keep praying, but God hasn't removed it from your life. You're tired and frustrated, and maybe you feel discouraged.

Still, you have to keep on pushing.

You have to push until your promise materializes. You have to keep on praying. Don't give up on your prayer. Don't give up on your children. Don't give up on what God can do in your life. Don't lose your faith over empty pursuits. God is still with you. God is saying, *"There are some things I need you to lose. And the first thing you have to do is let go of your pride."*

God wants to let his strength shine through your weakness. Embrace the very things that are hindering you. Use them as a testimony of what God can do through you. Let them remind you about that event that almost killed you but did not. That argument that almost destroyed your marriage but did not. That health crisis that almost broke you but could not.

Never forget what God has done for you. Never forget how God has saved you or delivered you. Don't become so Christian that you forget the grace and mercy of God in your life. Don't get so complacent that you don't worship the way you first worshiped.

God is saying, *"Don't stop worshiping me the way you worshiped when your breakthrough came. I am here to give you more, but I don't want you to be comfortable, so let me leave that thorn in your side to always remind you that you have made it because I have been with you."*

Embrace the thorn. Embrace the storm. You might be going through something, but God is saying, *"I am with you. You have to lose some things. You're working so hard to hold on, but just let go. I've got this."* Don't cling to all the toys weighing you down. God does not want you to stay there. He wants you to keep on pushing. And for you to keep on moving, you must throw off what's weighing you down. Sacrifice the very things in your life that hinder your relationship with God. You'll never know what you will gain until you're willing to lose everything for God!

PRAYING FOR MORE

God, you have been so faithful to me and provided for me in so many ways throughout my life—ways I couldn't see at the time but now see. Thank you for having more for me—more of what I truly long for—than all the things in this world that I sometimes chase after. I only want you, Lord, and I know that you alone can satisfy the hunger in my heart. Show me what I need to sacrifice, what I need to relinquish in my life and toss aside to grow closer to you. To you alone belong all the praise and glory for what you have done, what you're doing, and what you're about to do in my life. I love you, Lord. Amen.

Chapter 8

RISKING FOR MORE

Unless there is an element of risk in our exploit for
God, there is no need for faith.

—HUDSON TAYLOR

I visited Haiti in January of 2010, a week after the devastating earthquake there claimed more than one hundred thousand lives, injured just as many or more, and destroyed thousands of homes and businesses. Like so many others, our church immediately sent doctors, nurses, and anyone with medical training willing to go, along with supplies and as much food and bottled water as possible. But we also organized a group of volunteers willing to go and do all they could for the injured and suffering people who had just lost loved ones, homes, businesses—everything.

Landing in Santo Domingo, we boarded a rented van and began our journey east toward Port-au-Prince, close to the epicenter of the quake. The closer we got, the more difficult our journey became. The roads, which weren't so great before the disaster, looked like the surface of the moon, with huge, crater-like potholes every few yards. It was like being on an amusement-park ride. I prayed for our vehicle's suspension to last until we got to our destination, a rural village several miles from the capital.

We saw in every direction piles of debris and rubble, collapsed buildings, shattered walls, and crumbled asphalt. The air smelled of diesel fuel and decay. Homeless survivors, many of them children, huddled around makeshift fires and called out to us for help. Prepared for the worst, I still found conditions harsher than imagined. It felt like we had entered a war zone where the latest battle was still raging. My heart was broken for these people.

When we finally arrived at our destination, it was almost midnight, but hundreds of people had gathered there waiting for us. Time is meaningless when you have no food, no clean water, no home, no hospitals or doctors, nothing. Relief workers from the Red Cross and US military had not yet reached this remote village, so before we could even get off the bus, the awaiting crowd surrounded our vehicle, pounding on the sides. They were desperate.

Many of them had heard we were coming and had made superhuman efforts to get there. They had limped and crawled, arriving on foot or by donkey or in the back of flatbed pickup trucks. Their clothes were torn and smudged, and their eyes hollow. They looked not only helpless but hopeless.

Understandably, many people in our group were frightened by their volatile, almost violent reception to our arrival. I was trying to quiet everyone down and get our translator out of the bus to disperse the crowd. That's when a gentleman, a volunteer who was not from our church, leaned over to me and said, "Pastor Choco, we have to get out of here! We should give the food and supplies to the nearest military team and drive back to the airport."

I remember looking back at this man. It was as if everything around us had suddenly stopped. "We came here to save lives and make a difference," I told him. "When I said good-bye to my family this morning, I wondered if that was the last time I'd see them. We're here to serve, and that's what we're going to do." He nodded, but I could still see fear in his eyes.

I was just as afraid as that guy, so it wasn't his fear that bothered me; it was his presumption that what we were doing should be without risk. I don't know what he expected conditions to be like. Most of the time when we step out in faith and take a risk, we don't know what we're getting into.

When you and I experience God's more, we're also compelled to take risks so that others may experience it too. It's not easy, and often it takes us out of our comfort zone, but sacrificing ourselves for others brings us closer to the heart of Jesus. When we follow his example, we discover that risking more of ourselves usually leads to experiencing more of God.

> *When you and I experience God's more, we're also compelled to take risks so that others may experience it too.*

More Will Be Asked

I had been on many mission trips before and traveled frequently to developing countries where poverty, disease, and lack of clean water were the norm. Still, what I encountered in Haiti during that trip cut deep into my heart and caused me to reconsider many of the things that I—and most of us—consider to be problems. Problems like whether to trade in our car for a different one or when to remodel our kitchen pale in the face of everyday survival. It reminds me of the way a friend of mine refers to most people's complaints as "first-world problems"— issues that really aren't problems at all, only signs of living in an affluent, entitled culture.

As I witnessed in Haiti after the quake, there are problems, and then there are *real problems*. When your home gets leveled and your family is injured or killed beneath the rubble, now that's a problem. When your bones remain broken and you haven't eaten in days, the word *problem* no longer applies. I'm not trivializing or dismissing the very real problems in the United States and other developed nations. I'm just saying that even our poorest citizens would likely be considered rich by many of the suffering people in the world, such as the survivors I met in Haiti. We may not have all we want right now, but most of us have more than enough of what we truly need.

In addition to reminding me of the many, many blessings in my life, my time in Haiti also reminded me of what I'm called to do with the gifts God has entrusted to me. During my time there, I realized that being part of the solution to someone else's real problem is much more satisfying than solving any of my first-world problems. God has not given me more—more responsibility, more resources, more relationships—so that I can reach a comfortable plateau and rest on past accomplishments and present privileges. Nor has he given you more simply to enjoy it. Our enjoyment is just a secondary product of our primary goal of loving and serving others.

Once you're living for Christ and empowered by the Holy

Spirit, *risk* is simply another word for faith. In one of my favorite parables of Jesus, we find a story about risk and return. Usually called the parable of the talents (Matt. 25:14–30), this cautionary tale reminds us to invest what God has given us instead of just sitting on it.

The parable begins with a person going on a journey and delegating responsibility for his resources to three trusted team members. To the first he gave five bags of gold, to the second he gave two, and to the third he gave one, "each according to his ability," we're told (Matt. 25:15). When this man returns and asks for a report from his three lieutenants, he discovers that the first two had invested the resources they oversaw and produced a return. The third one, however, buried his one talent in the ground. While he claims to be afraid of risking his talent and his boss's disapproval, this excuse doesn't work. Risking the talent and having no return is preferable to playing it safe and burying it.

When you bury what God has given you, whether it's out of fear or selfishness, you guarantee there will be no dividends. Stepping out in faith and taking risks are inherent to the Christian life. Jesus said, "From everyone who has been given much, much will be demanded; and from the one who has been entrusted with much, much more will be asked" (Luke 12:48).

Steep Price of Obedience

I can think of no more powerful example of stepping out in faith and taking a risk than the life of Abraham. Earlier, in chapter 4, we explored the Hebrews 11 Faith Hall of Fame.

This passage offers us a who's who of people taking enormous risks and demonstrating tremendous faith in God. While it's no surprise to see Abraham listed there, I think the reasons the author has listed are significant.

Abraham lived a remarkable life that often required him to step out in faith and trust the Lord. Moving away from his homeland, changing his name, and not giving up on having a son are just a few that come to mind. In the Faith Hall of Fame, however, Abraham is noted for his most personal and heart-wrenching sacrifice:

> By faith Abraham, when God tested him, offered Isaac as a sacrifice. He who had embraced the promises was about to sacrifice his one and only son, even though God had said to him, "It is through Isaac that your offspring will be reckoned." Abraham reasoned that God could even raise the dead, and so in a manner of speaking he did receive Isaac back from death. (Heb. 11:17–19)

Here we see Abraham commended for his obedience and faith. Abraham did not know where the road would lead him, but he had so much faith in God that Abraham would do what seems unthinkable to us today. God had promised Abraham that he would be the forefather of a mighty nation. And don't forget that for the longest time, Abraham and his wife, Sarah, were unable to conceive a child. Then, finally, against all odds and human logic, when Abe was one hundred and Sarah was ninety, they conceived and had Isaac (Gen. 18). They knew faith is the substance and the evidence of things unseen.

Even with such great faith in God, Abraham still struggled

with his decision, I suspect. If we wonder why God would ask such a thing of a man who had followed God his whole life, surely Abraham did as well. Traveling up that mountain couldn't have been easy, knowing what he was going there to do. Surely Abraham was confused by God's request and wondered if he had heard the Lord correctly. He must have thought, *After all this time—decades—before God finally gave me a son, now he wants me to kill him as a sacrifice?* Certainly God's ways are above and beyond our ways, but this just didn't make sense. Why would God give Abraham what he longed for most, only to ask him to give it back?

We can't understand what that conversation must have been like or how Abraham felt about obeying God's instruction. But we do know two things: (1) Abraham was obedient and willing to do the hardest thing I can imagine someone having to do—give up a child; and (2) the writer of Hebrews tells us that this was a test, a way for God to strengthen Abraham's faith, and that Abraham passed this test.

We all have our Isaac—someone or something that means the world to us. I'm not saying that Abraham loved his son more than God and that's why God asked him to sacrifice Isaac. But I am saying that when we're reluctant to give up something dear to us, when the price of obedience requires more from us than we're used to giving, we stand at the threshold of risking more.

Ultimately, Abraham pleased God because he decided to place his plans in God's hands. Abraham relinquished his own desires and wishes and chose to follow God even when it seemed counter to everything he knew about God. Abraham's willingness pleased God and allowed him to discover more—specifically, a ram caught in a thicket nearby to sacrifice.

Sometimes people wonder if the ram would have appeared if Abraham had suddenly changed his mind about obeying God. But wondering about such possibilities only makes my head hurt, because in the end, it's still a matter of trust. There

are times—many times—when we're called to obey in the midst of doubts, uncertainty, fear, and danger. During such moments when we stand at a crossroad,

---
We must dare to hope for more when less is all around us.

---

we must risk trusting God for more than we can see, for more than what logic dictates, and for more than what others tell us to expect.

We must dare to hope for more when less is all around us.

More in the Moment

When have you experienced events in your life that just didn't make sense? How did you respond during those times? Maybe you lost your job unexpectedly or accidentally discovered your spouse had betrayed you. Perhaps you heard grim news from the doctor or struggled with a chronic illness. Every day people come face-to-face with totally unexpected, life-changing, devastatingly painful news. These losses leave them wondering how God could allow such a terrible thing to happen.

During such times of crisis and upheaval, it's human nature to try to take control of the situation and find a way to fix the problem. But when we hold tight and try to do it ourselves, we miss out on the blessings of more God has for us. Sacrificing our plans, dreams, and desires in the moment may feel like we're settling for less. But faith is trusting that no matter how much we might lose, if we have God, we always have more.

Throughout each season of my life, I would have missed many miraculous and joyful moments if I had refused to step out in faith and obey God. If I had insisted on being in law enforcement or sales instead of ministry, I might have enjoyed part of my life. By being obedient to God and sacrificing what I thought I wanted at the time, though, I invested in more than I could see or even imagine. And that's what faith is all about—not being able to see how God is going to do it but knowing he will make a way.

You and I live in a world with a lot of uncertainties. Most people I talk to worry about global concerns, such as helping others hit by natural disasters similar to the one in Haiti, as well as deeply personal worries, such as having money to pay the mortgage this month. And amid so many unknowns, so many problems and issues for which we are unable to see solutions, we can know one thing for sure: our Redeemer lives.

Most of us don't know when or how we are going to die, but we can know where we are headed after we leave this earth. We may not know the outcome of the next election, the next ball game, the next school year, the next legal dispute. But we can know that God is in control no matter how those other events might fall. Our hope is in him—not in our leaders or political parties, not in how many wins we have, not in how much money we have in our bank accounts.

But we must risk.

If you want more of God, if you want the things of God, then to get from here to there, you are going to have to take risks. And the price may be steep and the losses painful.

Friends may leave you. Family members might not want to talk to you. You won't be invited to office parties or neighborhood cookouts. Nobody invites me to parties anymore, and I love going to parties! But they think I might get there and start preaching. I may say things that are not what everyone wants to hear. And you know what? They're right! I might do those things. I want to be able to serve the Lord and walk with the Lord, worship the Lord and work for him, walk in the Spirit, walk in the light, walk in the Word of God, no matter where I am.

When we're committed to God this way, we risk losing people. We risk losing their fellowship and affection, their affirmation and attention. When you decide to follow the Bible, and not your friends, not Facebook, and not what's politically correct, be prepared for the world to hate you. But it really shouldn't bother us, because they hated Jesus first. We're not here on earth to make people happy. We're here to serve the Lord, to be stewards of all he gives us, to worship him.

What's the payoff when we're risking for more?

From the earliest era of human history, the search for significance has always been about intimacy, about fellowship, about communion with God. And the good news is that this is what he wants. God wants a relationship. He wants to talk to you. Just as he did with Adam, God wants to walk with you in the coolness of the day. And I'm not talking about walking with us as if we're his pets like we would walk our dogs! No, God wants to walk with us as intimate friends, as parent and child, as lover and beloved.

Sometimes we may say we want this deep, rich intimacy with God, when it actually scares us to death. We'd actually much prefer for it to be more like a casual walk around the block or a stroll in the park on a leash. So we keep him at arm's length instead of confronting our fears and laying them before him. We create defenses and place our trust in our own power or in money or in other people.

But we can't keep saying we want one thing and doing another. If we want God's more, then we must risk having less. We must risk making hard decisions.

Standing Up or Bowing Down

Abraham wasn't the only pillar of the faith we see in the Bible risking for more. Another of my favorite examples is Daniel, God's prophet who lived most of his life as a prisoner of war in Babylon. As if being defeated by violent, immoral foreigners wasn't bad enough, Daniel frequently found himself in the crosshairs, caught between obeying God and risking his life or obeying a pagan king and risking his faith.

Daniel didn't have a lot of support among his own people. Their rebellion against God is what got them in trouble in the first place. After David and Solomon had reigned, Israel split along geographical and tribal lines. Within a few generations, the ten northern tribes of Israel began abandoning their faith in God and started worshiping idols.

God wasn't pleased. So he warned them repeatedly, but the words of his prophets fell on deaf ears. Eventually their disobedience brought God to the place of extreme measures: allowing their enemy the Assyrians to conquer all ten tribes in the northern kingdom (see 2 Kings 17:16–23).

Daniel, however, lived in the southern kingdom, comprised of Judah and the smaller tribe of Benjamin. Even after watching the defeats of their northern kinsmen, these southerners continued drifting farther away from God. Once again he began issuing the same kind of warnings through his prophets—Jeremiah, Habakkuk, and Zephaniah. And once again, their words went unheeded.

So God allowed another foreign nation to defeat them and take them captive. Under the leadership of King Nebuchadnezzar, the Babylonians had already conquered Assyria and Egypt, so claiming Judah and destroying Jerusalem wasn't too hard. After looting the temple there, they took the entire Hebrew nation captive and brought them back to Babylon to live as slaves.

Most scholars think Daniel was probably around sixteen when he was brought to Babylon along with thousands of other enslaved Jews. Daniel's situation was about as tough as it gets. There was no army to come rescue him and the Hebrew people, no leader to strike a deal with the Babylonian king—nothing.

From a human vantage point, Daniel had no hope. He never despaired, though, even in the midst of all the tests, temptations, and torture from his captors. When ordered to eat the rich foods and wines of the court, which were often leftovers from offerings to pagan gods, Daniel instead asked if he and his young Hebrew friends could drink water and eat vegetables. His captors agreed and were surprised to discover that their prisoners were even stronger and healthier than natives on the Babylonian diet.

Perhaps the greatest test came when Daniel and his friends were pressured to bow down to an idol created by the king.

Nebuchadnezzar not only erected a ninety-foot statue made of gold, but he wanted everyone to fall on their knees and worship when his royal band struck up a tune. Daniel and his friends had no way out of the situation with their faith intact. The king promised to turn up the heat, literally, if they didn't comply: "Whoever does not fall down and worship will immediately be thrown into a blazing furnace" (Dan. 3:6).

Rather than compromise their faith in the living God by bowing before the king's twenty-four-karat creation, they made a stand. They risked their lives rather than their faith.

> Shadrach, Meshach and Abednego replied to him, "King Nebuchadnezzar, we do not need to defend ourselves before you in this matter. If we are thrown into the blazing furnace, the God we serve is able to deliver us from it, and he will deliver us from Your Majesty's hand. But even if he does not, we want you to know, Your Majesty, that we will not serve your gods or worship the image of gold you have set up." (Dan. 3:16–18)

Now that's keeping your cool! In our culture today, many forces pull at us to compromise our convictions and to forfeit our faith. I love how clear-cut these three guys made it. They didn't beg for mercy, plot a rebellion, organize a boycott, or condemn the king for building his idol and making such a ridiculous decree. As we see in their response, they didn't defend their decision at all—period! They just said, "We're not going to bow."

They trusted the Lord to rescue them—and here's what I absolutely love—but even if he didn't, they said they still would not regret their decision. Sure enough, the three of them were cast in the furnace—right after it was stoked to be as hot as possible—but they emerged without even a scorch mark. God honored their fireproof faith and protected them from harm.

Daniel repeatedly faced life-threatening ordeals from his Babylonian captors. You may recall a famous incident involving a lions' den. Time after time, Daniel remained steadfast, risking his safety and very life, to remain faithful and obedient to his God.

We're told that in response to Daniel's faith, God demonstrated his supernatural power to honor the one who honored him (1 Sam. 2:30). Consistently displaying humility and strength over the next seventy years, Daniel earned respect from *four* different Babylonian emperors. The last one, Cyrus, granted the Jewish people their freedom so they could return home.

Swimming Upstream

The call to take a stand for God's truth in the midst of threatening circumstances is nothing new. You and I are frequently confronting the same challenges Daniel faced centuries ago in Babylon: how can we remain anchored in God's Word and obedient to his truth in the midst of so many cultural tides flooding the circumstances of our everyday lives? Do we make a stand and refuse to engage with people who believe differently than we do, often swimming upstream against their current? Or do we just shrug and go with the flow?

Daniel's example reminds us that there is another way, a path through the middle. You can remain strong in your faith, refusing to compromise and bow to cultural idols, while respecting and being respected by others around you. In addition to respect, Daniel also demonstrated that avoiding the extremes requires humility, compassion, and dependence on God. We can only reflect who God truly is, both his holy righteousness and his gracious love, by relying on his Spirit to guide us.

Daniel modeled the kind of response to his culture that I attempt to bring to mine. As a pastor in the heart of Chicago, I have often been faced with cultural conflicts that required me to take action while maintaining respect for the government leaders' authority and others' points of view. Several years ago I agreed to participate in a boycott to protest the city's unfair policies and hiring practices for Hispanic teachers, administrators, and law enforcers.

I had always considered our mayor at the time a friend of mine, but I had to be willing to risk that friendship to do what I knew was right. So I gathered dozens of other pastors and community leaders from across Chicagoland to join me in making our voices heard. And you know what? The following month, the city hired five new Hispanic police commanders!

I remember another situation a while back when the city proposed launching a new high school just for gay, lesbian, and transgender youth. I quickly realized I had a choice to make: remain silent and remove myself from the issue or speak up about the problem I had with organizing a school this way. I knew whatever I said or did would be tough, and it was. When I spoke out against the school, many accused me of hating gay people and condemning them.

As a result, I had to work extra hard to make it clear that I seek to love, understand, and serve all people—including homosexuals. The school ordinance didn't pass, but the tension it created in our community intensified. So a few months later, when I was being considered for a city council position in Chicago, a number of prominent LGBT leaders spoke out against me. Instead of lashing back or trying to defend myself, I did something that I knew came from the Lord: I met with as many of them as possible in a restaurant to discuss our perspectives.

Many people from church offered to go with me, and some couldn't believe I was willing to go to this meeting alone, but I didn't want to risk intimidating those in attendance. I thought the best way to disarm the situation was for them to see my vulnerability before them. And of course, it was uncomfortable and a little scary because I didn't know what to expect or what others might say or do there.

But I also knew God was with me, and he loves all people— including those who don't abide by his guidelines on sexuality and marriage. Like so many people, they are alone, hurting, and often have not been loved well by people in the church. So a few hours of my discomfort was a small price to pay for the possibility of a deeper human connection with people who didn't like me. For the opportunity for me to know them better and for them to know Jesus better, the risk was more than worth it.

Skilled Sailors

It may feel like our one voice or individual actions don't make a difference in huge issues or complicated circumstances. But they do. We must be like those three amigos who willingly jumped in the furnace rather than denounce their faith in God. We must be willing to risk what we're called to do and leave the results to God.

When you decide to serve the Lord and break away—from family, from friends, from culture—the break is not going to be pretty. But if you want to

> *We must be willing to risk what we're called to do and leave the results to God.*

mature in your faith and experience deeper intimacy with God—if you really want your life to count and you want to experience the fullness that more of God brings—you have to risk more.

Someone once said, "A calm sea does not produce a skilled sailor." That person was right. If you want to be a skilled sailor, you must face a storm. If everything is calm in your life, you don't really build skills or increase your experience. You really don't build character or grow stronger. You really don't build your faith if everything remains smooth sailing all the time.

> *Someone once said, "A calm sea does not produce a skilled sailor." That person was right.*

If you want to walk on water, then you have to get out of your boat and fix your eyes on Jesus. Unless you're willing to lose it all, unless you're willing to leave the shore and give up the comfort and safety of solid ground, you won't find God in the deep waters of life's storms. If you want to live a life of abundance, adventure, and fulfillment, if you want to experience miracles, then it's time to step forward. Less playing it safe, more risking it all.

PRAYING FOR MORE

God, forgive me for playing it safe sometimes. I get scared, Lord, and worry about my own safety and comfort more than the needs of others. Give me your strength and courage—the kind I see in Abraham and Daniel—to risk losing what is temporary in order to gain what is eternal. Attune my heart to your Spirit and empower me with your love when I'm called to take a stand for truth or to speak out against injustice or oppression. I don't want a shallow, superficial faith, Lord. I want to be your "skilled sailor" and wade into the deeper waters of sacrificing my life for others. Thank you for leading the way. Amen.

Chapter 9

THE BLESSINGS OF A LIFE WITH MORE

*Be happy when God answers your prayer, but be
happier when you are an answer to others' prayers.*

—ANONYMOUS

H is Majesty will see you now," said the solemn brown-
skinned young man in a long white tunic. "You will not
look at the *Moro Naba*. Ask your questions through the king's
translator. This way please."

It sounded like an awkward way to have a conversation,
but I experienced many new and unusual customs during that
mission trip to Africa. Regardless of the different situations,
I always did my best to show respect to the native people I was
privileged to meet. And there I was, about to greet a real king
in his royal palace in the windswept nation of Burkina Faso, just
north of Ghana along Africa's Ivory Coast.

This landlocked country is roughly the size of Colorado and
home to over 15 million people, about half of whom belong to

the indigenous Mossi tribe. Formerly known as Upper Volta, the nation's name was changed to Burkina Faso, loosely translated as "the land of upright people," in 1984. Although it operates as a modern republic with a president, government leadership has been tumultuous since it declared its independence from France, its colonial parent, in 1960. A stabilizing force within the violent upheavals and military coups, however, has been the Mossi king, called by the title Moro Naba, "head of the world."

My first exposure to the current Moro Naba, King Baongo II, occurred outside his palace in a dusty courtyard within the capital city of Ouagadougou. The king performs a traditional ceremony each morning demonstrating both the history and power of his position. First, he emerges from the palace gate wearing a deep red robe and brandishing a long sword. As he strides toward a waiting stallion bedecked in red, blue, and gold finery, the king is intercepted by one of several dozen courtiers who are all lined up before him.

His lieutenant then begs the king not to declare war and is soon joined by other members of the court. A cannon is fired—it's incredibly loud for 7:00 a.m.—before the king departs, only to reappear moments later clad in a bright white robe with empty hands, symbolically bringing peace to his people. Many tourists were there that warm, humid morning when we watched the ceremony, but many locals attended as well.

The king then greeted various people in the crowd, which was considered a real honor. Because we stood out as visitors from the United States, one of the king's courtiers told us the king would like to receive us in his royal palace later that day. We were honored, of course, and quickly agreed.

Standing before him a few hours later, I maintained the

strange protocol of not looking at him, or he at me. Instead, we spoke through his interpreting aide. We exchanged formal greetings and pleasantries, and then the king inquired about our reason for being in Burkina Faso.

"Tell your king that I am here as an ambassador of the kingdom of heaven," I said to the interpreter. "Tell him that I serve a king named Jesus Christ."

After the translator repeated my message to the king, he nodded and looked directly at me, breaking the traditional practice. "Would you pray for me?" he asked.

The dynamic between us melted from odd formality into one of mutual warmth and trust, like two old friends meeting up. I looked him in the eye, told him how happy I would be to pray for him, and then stepped forward to place my hands on him. If the reaction of his staff was any indication, having a visitor touch their king was clearly not something that usually happened. But the king seemed pleased as I prayed, asking God's blessings on him and his leadership.

We continued to chat, and the king asked if I would like to tour the rest of his royal residence, including his private rooms. We then strolled from room to room while he shared—in broken English as well as through his interpreter—about the various artifacts, paintings, and weapons displayed. The tribal history of the Mossi people, represented by a variety of historical displays, fascinated me.

Toward the end of my tour, the king then led me into a room that, based on its design and security, clearly held valuable, cherished objects—his collection of sports memorabilia. The king loved sports, especially soccer, and had numerous jerseys, balls, and championship banners from his favorite teams and players. As a lifelong baseball fan, I realized it was one more thing we had in common.

This extended, spontaneous visit with the king was a blessing from the Lord, far more than anything I could have tried to arrange myself. I treasure that experience as a powerful reminder: when you trust God for more, his blessings always follow.

Blessed Are the Blessers

Bless, *blessed*, and *blessing* are overused but misunderstood by most people. Many Christians talk about the blessings in their lives, but those around them may have no idea what a blessing really is. And perhaps there's only so much others can understand without knowing the source of all blessings, the living God. As the Bible tells us, "Every good and perfect gift is from above, coming down from the Father of the heavenly lights, who does not change like shifting shadows" (James 1:17).

In God's Word, we find three words in the original languages, Hebrew and Greek, that we usually translate as "bless" or "blessing." God makes a promise to Abraham to bless him and make his name great, blessing those who bless him and cursing those who curse him (Gen. 12:1–3). The word used originally is *barak*, which literally means to kneel before someone or something. In this context, the meaning points to the commitment God and Abraham made to one another. While Abraham likely kneeled, literally, in worship, God revealed himself and made a promise to Abraham.

We find another, perhaps more familiar, connotation of

blessing used in Psalms and Proverbs. The Hebrew word *esher* is typically rendered, implying joy and happiness—the feelings we probably think of when considering ourselves blessed. In fact, the Psalms begin with this word, "Blessed is the one who does not walk in step with the wicked" (Ps. 1:1), showing contrast between the righteous who follow God and the wicked who continue to sin and mock.

The Greek word used in the New Testament, *makarios*, is similar in meaning and conveys a sense of happiness, delight, and fulfillment. We see it famously translated as "blessed" in Jesus's Sermon on the Mount, the part usually called the Beatitudes because each statement begins, "Blessed are the . . ." (Matt. 5:1–12). Virtually all of Christ's proclamations here again set up a contrast—this time between suffering conditions such as poverty, loss, injustice, and persecution and yet still enjoying the blessings of spiritual peace and contentment in the midst of them.

When we consider being blessed or counting our blessings, we often think of the material, physical, concrete items we enjoy, such as our house, a warm bed, good food, clean water, a car that runs, clothes to wear, and so on. These tangible manifestations are all surely blessings from the Lord, but the way Jesus uses this word in the Beatitudes also encompasses something spiritual, invisible, eternal, and self-contained. Despite our external circumstances, we are genuinely blessed as God's children and followers of Jesus Christ.

I suspect the confusion about blessings occurs because we tend to focus on what we can see while God focuses on what goes unseen, on what's in our hearts. In the Old Testament when the prophet Samuel is searching for the next king of Israel, God reminds him not to judge a book by its cover: "The LORD does not look at the things people look at. People look at the outward appearance, but the LORD looks at the heart" (1 Sam. 16:7).

With this distinction in mind, I suspect some of our problem in asking God for material blessings is that we don't often consider our true motives. Why are we asking him for a new car when the old one runs just fine? Do we really need a bigger house so we can accommodate more guests, or do we want to feel better about our status in the neighborhood? Are we asking for more money so we can feel secure or so we can use it as a resource for serving others and advancing God's kingdom?

While it's easy for me to present either end of our motivational spectrum, most human motives are usually mixed. We want to serve God, but we also like the security that comes from paying our bills on time and replacing the washer when it breaks. There's nothing wrong with the enjoyment of any of the material blessings God gives us. It becomes a problem, however, when we start to feel entitled and try to treat God like a divine machine. You know, put in your prayers and other Christian behaviors and out comes whatever you ask for.

Of course, that's not the way blessings work—especially not in the economy of God's more. There's definitely a relationship between our obedience to God and the blessings we receive.

But our obedience to him should never be motivated by what we will get out of it— only what we can give him in return for all he has given us.

But our obedience to him should never be motivated by what we will get out of it—only what we can give him in return for all he has given us.

Trust and Obey

One of the hardest parts of our Christian walk is to stay obedient. It's tough because true obedience is not about what we should do, or even want to do, but what we actually do. Many people want the blessings that come from an obedient life, but what makes obedience count is a faith that's not easily shaken. As Paul reminds us, "Therefore, my beloved brethren, be steadfast, immovable, always abounding in the work of the Lord, knowing that your labor is not in vain in the Lord" (1 Cor. 15:58 NKJV).

I love Paul's choice of the word "steadfast" here to describe this firm, solid faith. This kind of faith has both consistency and continuity. It's steady trust in God even when life's storms toss and turn our circumstances. A faith that might bend during hard times but never breaks. A loving trust in God that fuels our obedience to him even when we don't like it, understand it, or know how we'll do it.

It's this kind of faith we saw listed in the Hebrews 11 Faith Hall of Fame. The kind that compelled Abel to offer his very best to God, that motivated Noah to build the ark even when everyone thought he was crazy, that empowered Moses to confront Pharaoh and lead his people's exodus from Egypt. It's the steadfast kind of faith seen in Abraham's willingness to sacrifice Isaac. If not for their obedience, and the obedience of so many other followers of God, they wouldn't have experienced all that God had for them.

What if Abraham had refused and said, "Sorry, God, but that's too much! I'm not giving up something I waited my whole life to receive from you." What if Isaac had pushed his father away and said, "Dad, you're crazy! I'm not going to let you sacrifice me!" and left the altar. They would have left the mountaintop and never experienced the provision of God because they left too soon. Any time we rationalize, justify, or outright refuse to obey God, we miss out on some blessing he wanted to give us.

And in our crazy-fast world, we often move too fast to maintain the steadfast faith and patience that obeying God requires. We have grown accustomed to immediate gratification everywhere in our lives, from our Wi-Fi coverage to microwaveable meals to online shopping. But God's timing can't be rushed. He is with us for the long haul—not just the two hours we try to squeeze him into on Sundays.

This impatience leads to taking matters into our own hands and trying to make something happen for ourselves. Even with the disciplines we practice to grow closer to God, we sometimes adopt a consumer attitude and refuse to continue if they don't make us feel the way we want to feel. We get off the altar where God is calling us to sacrifice our own wishes because we refuse to wait. We think, *Well, my healing is not happening fast enough,* or *I've been reading the Word all month, and I'm still not feeling the joy of the Lord like I should.*

So often God tells us, *"Stay put. Keep going. Be still before me."* He wants our faith to be steadfast and unshakable. He wants us committed to doing his work because his requests of us have eternal value. They may not satisfy our desires for more in the moment. But they last much, much longer and reap rewards that last forever.

I don't know about you, but I like knowing that what I do each day has eternal value. I want to make sure that if I'm going to invest my time, energy, and money in something, my investment is going to have eternal results. Paul said we should be "always abounding in the work of the Lord" (1 Cor. 15:58 NKJV). That word "abounding" means to go above and beyond, to give more than required, to overdo it. It's not just scraping by or doing the bare minimum to fulfill an obligation or responsibility. It's giving all you have, 110 percent every time.

Jesus gave all he had for us by leaving heaven to die a painful death on the cross for our salvation. The only natural response to such a sacrificial outpouring of love is to give all we have as well. As we're told in Scripture, "We love because he first loved us" (1 John 4:19).

Blessonomics 101

Scripture also makes it clear that God blesses us, not so we can live in greed and indulgent pleasure, but so that we can bless others. Initially in Genesis we see God doing all the blessing—in chapter 1 he blessed what he created, in chapter 9 he blessed Noah after the flood. But with Abraham, God partners with humanity so that his followers can use their blessings to bless others. He told Abraham, "I will make you into a great nation, and I will bless you; I will make your name great, and *you will be a blessing*." God's radical blessing on Abraham concludes with the promise that "all peoples on earth will be blessed *through you*" (Gen. 12:2–3, emphasis added).

When his Spirit dwells in us, God, the ultimate blesser, passes on the privilege of blessing others to us. Our Father gives good gifts to us, his children, so that we can give good gifts to those around us. And God has given everyone different gifts to be used for the benefit of others. In his Word we're told, "Each of you should use whatever gift you have received to serve others, as faithful stewards of God's grace in its various forms. If anyone speaks, they should do so as one who speaks the very words of God. If anyone serves, they should do so with the strength God provides, so that in all things, God may be praised through Jesus Christ. To him be the glory and the power for ever and ever. Amen" (1 Peter 4:10–11).

You can be a blessing to others simply by speaking kind words, by volunteering your time in the ministry, by giving of your financial resources, by sharing your possessions, by giving food, and simply by sharing your testimony of God's grace and goodness in your life. If you're committed to knowing God and following Jesus and living by the Spirit, you just have to show up!

We always have an opportunity to bless others—every hour of every day. That's why we're here. Even if it's just listening to someone share their pain or buying a meal for someone who's hungry. A kind gesture to a coworker. A thoughtful gift for a family member. An anonymous donation to a neighbor in need. Praying for God to provide for someone else's need. The more we seek to bless others, the more God will allow us to take part in their blessing.

And in the process, we're blessed in return. As you empty yourself and pour into somebody's life, God pours into you! You're never without God. He says, *"Go ahead—give it all. I'll fill you. But you have to empty yourself. I can't give you more if your hands are full trying to hold on to what you have."* When we empty ourselves, we become conduits and open a current flowing right back through us. We pour into people, and then God pours more into us so we can pour more into more people.

We're told, "Whoever brings blessing will be enriched, and one who waters will himself be watered" (Prov. 11:25 ESV). When you give, you're not left empty—you give and then God refills you and replenishes you. You can always give everything you have, because God delights in filling you up again. Never pass up an opportunity to bless someone else, because when you do, you'll miss out on the blessing you would have received in the place of the blessing you gave.

> *God can't give you more if your hands are full trying to hold on to what you have.*

That's how "blessonomics" works. God has empowered us to bless those around us with his power. Again, we are blessed not to hoard his gifts for our own selfish gain but to bless others with what he has given us. This has nothing to do with the "prosperity gospel," the name-it-and-claim-it belief that God's favor always results in material wealth, which some people try to pass off as God's truth. While we will reap what God has given us to sow, we don't do it just to receive a bumper crop. We do it out of loving obedience and the opportunity to give God glory as we share the good news and serve others.

Did You Hear Something?

There's a curious story, more like a chapter from military history, in the Old Testament that illustrates the power of sharing what you have been given. It begins during a time when a terrible famine had struck Israel, a disaster so severe that mothers even ate their children (2 Kings 6:24–30). As if matters couldn't get any worse, the Syrian army had surrounded Jerusalem and made camp, waiting until the famine had weakened enough people to ensure their conquest. That's the big picture, but our story focuses on four guys who found themselves trapped in no-man's-land:

> Now there were four leprous men at the entrance of the gate; and they said to one another, "Why are we sitting here until we die? If we say, 'We will enter the city,' the famine is in the city, and we shall die there. And if we sit here, we die also. Now therefore, come, let us surrender to the army of the Syrians. If they keep us alive, we shall live; and if they kill us, we shall only die."
>
> And they rose at twilight to go to the camp of the Syrians; and when they had come to the outskirts of the Syrian camp, to their surprise no one was there. For the Lord had caused the army of the Syrians to hear the noise of chariots and the noise of horses—the noise of a great army; so they said to one another, "Look, the king of Israel has hired against us the kings of the Hittites and the kings of the Egyptians to attack us!" Therefore they arose and fled at twilight, and left the camp intact—their tents, their horses, and their donkeys—and they fled for their lives.
>
> And when these lepers came to the outskirts of the camp, they went into one tent and ate and drank, and carried from it silver and gold and clothing. (2 Kings 7:3–8 NKJV)

Leprosy was a terrible, often fatal disease caused by a bacterial infection. Causing extensive nerve damage and disfigurement to the body, leprosy was highly contagious, which meant people suffering from it were often feared, shunned, and quarantined. It seems logical that these four lepers had been placed outside the city walls to protect residents' health, especially since everyone was weak from the famine. So these guys were thinking out loud about their plight and realizing they were caught between a rock and a hard place, literally, a famine-plagued city and a hostile foreign army.

These guys knew that if they went back into the city, they would starve to death because no one had any food. On the other hand, if they left the gate, they risked having the Syrian soldiers kill them on sight. And if the four lepers did nothing, they would starve to death where they were. It was a horrible lose-lose-lose situation. But one of them said, "Hey, we at least have a shot if we surrender to the Syrians. Maybe they'll have pity on us and give us something to eat. Even if they kill us, we'll die faster than we would sitting here starving to death. It's our only play."

What happened next shows a playful side to God in the way he provided for these four lepers. They mustered up enough courage and strength to face the Syrians, only to discover that their camp was deserted. And why did the Syrians rush to leave what appeared to be a sure win for them? We're told the Lord caused the Syrians to hear some frightening sound effects—marching feet, whinnying horses, chariot wheels turning, voices shouting.

The Syrians panicked because, based on what they heard, they assumed the Israelites had enlisted the Hittites *and* the

Egyptians to defend their city. So the lepers had the whole place to themselves! Notice it wasn't anything the lepers—or anyone else—arranged; the Lord caused it to happen for them. This miracle was done by God and God alone. He removed their enemies, but they didn't know this until they stepped out in faith. When they took the risk to pursue the only option they had, they discovered what God had done.

But they had to step out in faith to discover the blessings of more.

Spread the Word

Their story doesn't end there, of course. After these four guys had stuffed themselves with prime rib, Chicago-style pizza, and the Windy City's finest hot dogs, and washed everything down with a gallon of root beer; and after they had plundered the vault and jewelry counter from one tent and were about to go back for more, they stopped in their tracks. They couldn't keep something this good to themselves.

One of them said, "This isn't right, guys. We hit the jackpot and just enjoyed the buffet while there's a whole city full of people starving to death. We can't keep this good news to ourselves—surely we'd be punished if we didn't share this bounty!" (2 Kings 7:9, my paraphrase). Sure enough, they went back and spread the word about the buffet of blessings waiting in the vacant Syrian camp.

When we experience the goodness of the Lord, we find ourselves feeling just like these lepers—eager to share the good news and help others experience the abundant life we're enjoying. As Christians, we know the power of the gospel in our lives, the way God has forgiven our sins, and the way his Spirit guides our lives. This is the ultimate good news! We're not only commanded by Jesus to share it (Matt. 28:16–20), but we should be bursting at the seams to tell others what he has done in our lives. This is more than paying it forward—it's exploding it forward!

How can we keep quiet about a God who loves us enough to send his Son to die for us? How can we not tell others about how much more our Father has given us than we ever imagined possible?

The only reason I can come up with is that we're not enjoying the spiritual abundance of God's presence in our lives. Are you enjoying what God has done for you and is doing for you on a daily basis? You're not able to share unless you enjoy it yourself. And if you're not enjoying, then why not?

Please understand the spiritual significance of this—the Enemy wants people to think that he is all-powerful, when that is not the truth at all. God already pushed back the gates of hell! Jesus defeated the power of death. No enemy can rise against you. Not one. And yet we walk around scared, uncertain, anxious.

Why? Because we don't realize that God has already vanquished the Enemy and opened the gates of heaven. Our heavenly Father wants to bless us with all that we need to enjoy the life he created us to live. If you know this and have already experienced his power in your life, then you can no longer remain silent. In his letter to the Romans, Paul reminded his readers of this ultimate blessing, one David also pointed out in Psalms: "Blessed are those whose transgressions are forgiven, whose sins are covered. Blessed is the one whose sin the Lord will never count against them" (Rom. 4:7–8).

I hope that reading those words makes you want to shout "Hallelujah!" and jump up and down. *It should.* Blessed is the person against whom the Lord will not count their sin. That is the ultimate blessing, that our sins have been forgiven, that we have been delivered. There is no bondage in our lives. We have received the greatest blessing possible, and God now wants us to share it the same way those four lepers told the Israelites about the bounty awaiting them.

Where the Water Is

When our lives reflect the beauty of God's holiness and joy, people will say, "What's up with you? I want what you have!" When our actions demonstrate the servant heart of Jesus, others will ask, "Why are you doing that? And why do you seem so happy doing that?" When our voices praise the Lord who saved us, who loves us and gives us life, those around us say, "Introduce me to this God you know—I don't think he sounds like I thought he did."

An African proverb warns, "There is only one crime worse than murder on the desert, and that is to know where the water is and not tell." Think about how many thirsty people you know—men and women, boys and girls, coworkers, friends, relatives. They're looking for more in their lives—more hope, more meaning, more significance.

And you have Living Water to give them.

God has given us his only Son and blessed us with the

greatest gift of salvation. And he wants to keep on blessing us as we practice blessing others with the abundance he has entrusted to us. The Lord tells each of us, "I will save you, and you shall be a blessing. Do not fear, let your hands be strong" (Zech. 8:13 NKJV).

So what has God placed in your hands to do? What has God assigned for you to do with what he has given you? He has dropped it in no one else's hands but yours.

> *An African proverb warns, "There is only one crime worse than murder on the desert, and that is to know where the water is and not tell."*

Someone is waiting to be blessed, for God's glory, with what you have in your life right now. God has purposed you to be a blessing. May God begin to work in you right now. May God begin to put someone in your mind right now that you and you alone can bless in a mighty way.

Never forget: you have been ordained to be a blessing. God has partnered with you. God has empowered you. God pours into you so you can share the blessing. He saved us so we can save others. You'll experience more blessings than you ever imagined if you're willing to live in the fullness of God's more!

PRAYING FOR MORE

Father, thank you so much for reminding me that you have purposed me to be a blessing to everyone around me. Using the abundance of abilities, talents, and resources that you have entrusted to me, I can now be a conduit of your mercy, grace, joy, and love to those in need. You saved me so that I can speak, with my words and even louder by my actions, the power of Jesus Christ to forgive sins and change lives. Everything I have, Lord, comes from you—my family, my home, my job, my money, my health, everything. I praise you and thank you for how you have blessed me in so many ways. I give all that I have back to you now, Lord, to use for your kingdom. Guide me and direct me and show me how I can use my blessings to bless others. Here's my life—I am yours. Amen.

Chapter 10

THE FULLNESS OF A LIFE WITH MORE

Contentment is natural wealth; luxury is artificial poverty.

—SOCRATES

I f you know me, then you know I love Chicago. Whether I'm people watching on Michigan Avenue with its Magnificent Mile of fancy shops, designer boutiques, and trendy restaurants, or visiting with friends in graffiti-covered communities, I draw energy from the vibe of my city. The Loop, Lake Michigan, Navy Pier, Union Station, the "L," Grant Park, O'Hare Airport, and Wrigley Field, along with communities surrounding my home and church, Wicker Park, Logan Square, and Buck Town—these are just a few of the many tiles in the beautifully complex mosaic that is the Windy City.

Chicago is part of me. Naturally, I have strong opinions about what we do well. We have the best deep-dish pizza in the world—my favorite is simply cheese and sausage and a buttery crust at least an inch thick. We have the Art Institute with world-renowned works by Van Gogh, Picasso, and Monet. We're dedicated to our sports teams: the Bulls and Bears, Blackhawks and White Sox, and of course the Cubs, for whom I no longer have to apologize or defend my support, thanks to a recent World Series championship—thank you, Jesus!

Chicago has it all, and I especially love our people—some of the most vibrant, colorful, and diverse people you'll meet anywhere. Most give warm, Midwestern kindness, but like any city our size, we have some residents who come across as rude and too busy for small talk. I've been blessed to travel around the world and encounter some truly extraordinary people and amazing places, but I always come home to Chicago.

Just because I love my city, however, doesn't mean I'm not aware of its faults and flaws. We have our share of problems, and some of them only seem to get worse. The one that disturbs me most is the dramatic disparity between those perched on top and those crawling at ground level, the powerful and the powerless. There are people renting storage units in the suburbs because they ran out of room in their three-story homes, and there are people pushing all their worldly belongings in a Walgreens shopping cart.

I've seen too many senseless tragedies unfold because some of us were too busy to care, to help, to share what we have. I've witnessed events in my city that didn't have to happen but did—gang wars, drive-by shootings that kill innocent children, addicts and junkies starving under park benches, racism and police brutality, girls and young women selling their bodies, homeless families struggling to stay together. While we're busy working late, driving the carpool, running to the mall, or making dinner reservations, other people all around us are desperately in need.

I know problems and solutions are not clear-cut. And it's not a sin to work hard and provide well for our families or to go out and enjoy ourselves in a nice restaurant. Still, I'm haunted by Jesus's words and actions, by the compassionate servant's heart he always displayed in his encounters with people—especially those in need. The poor, the sick, the brokenhearted, the grieving, beggars and lepers, prostitutes and tax collectors, widows and orphans, failures and fishermen.

So as much as I love Chicago, there's still more we must do. And no matter where you live, you can't forget the people in need.

Not if you want to experience the fullness that comes from living in God's more.

Eat, Drink, and Be Merry

The people in Jesus's day were no different than us—often focused on their definition of more instead of God's. Sometimes we don't even realize that's what we're doing, and then we end up asking God for our notion of more. Instead, we receive his. Christ faced this very situation once when he was teaching and someone in the crowd asked for his help with a very earthly minded problem:

> Someone in the crowd said to him, "Teacher, tell my brother to divide the inheritance with me."
> Jesus replied, "Man, who appointed me a judge or an

arbiter between you?" Then he said to them, "Watch out! Be on your guard against all kinds of greed; life does not consist in an abundance of possessions."

And he told them this parable: "The ground of a certain rich man yielded an abundant harvest. He thought to himself, 'What shall I do? I have no place to store my crops.'

"Then he said, 'This is what I'll do. I will tear down my barns and build bigger ones, and there I will store my surplus grain. And I'll say to myself, "You have plenty of grain laid up for many years. Take life easy; eat, drink and be merry."'

"But God said to him, 'You fool! This very night your life will be demanded from you. Then who will get what you have prepared for yourself?'

"This is how it will be with whoever stores up things for themselves but is not rich toward God." (Luke 12:13–21)

With thousands of people standing before him, Jesus had just delivered a message aimed at his disciples (Luke 12:1) when a very unique teaching opportunity arose. This guy in the crowd yelled a personal request, one I'm sure he felt passionately about and wanted Jesus to take seriously. His situation reminds me of two kids fighting over the last cookie and then the loser tattling to Mom or Dad, asking them to intervene and split the cookie evenly. But Jesus wasn't willing to play this man's game and give the final word on who got what.

He basically said, "Do I look like Judge Judy to you? Why should I arbitrate your inheritance with your brother?" And the Lord could have stopped there with the guy leaving upset because Jesus wouldn't do what this man wanted. But Christ knew how to read between the lines better than anyone who has ever walked this earth. He knew what was motivating the man to ask for help—greed.

The man asked for an external physical blessing, but Jesus's response was based on the internal condition of this guy's heart. Jesus saw an opportunity and used it as a springboard to tell the crowd a parable, an earthly story with a heavenly meaning. He knew that many times we ask God for physical blessings in our lives when we're not ready spiritually to handle them. Our motives are limited to an earthly, temporary perspective instead of a heavenly, eternal viewpoint.

Sometimes we ask for our own gain, pleasure, comfort, and convenience without considering the needs of others or the impact on them if we were to receive what we asked for. The parable Jesus told remains just as relevant today as it did then—and as I think about how many storage facilities I see while driving around Chicago, it may be more timely than ever!

Jesus's little story starts well enough—a rich person receives a windfall, and suddenly they're richer than they've ever been. The only problem is that they don't have enough room to store all their money. And that leads to the only logical solution to such a problem—tear down the vaults and storage facilities currently in use and build bigger ones! Once this new construction is completed, they can kick back and enjoy the good life as they eat, drink, and be merry. Who knows, they might even get their own reality TV series to showcase how rich they are!

If the story ended there, we might say, "Sounds good— what a wonderful story with a happy ending." Some of us might even think we can relate because we know that we too have been so blessed in our lives. "I have an overflow of blessings in my life," we say. "I can sit back and just chill, enjoying the surplus, the good life. That's what God wants, right? For me to live the good life?"

But the story didn't end there. God entered the picture and told this rich person, *"You fool! This very night your life will be demanded from you. Then what difference does it make how rich you are or how much stuff you have? Who's going to get it then? Not you!"* It's about the most alarming wake-up call a person could have! But it's one that we all need to remember on a daily basis, shifting our focus from ourselves to others, from right now to forevermore.

Just as he addressed the rich person in the parable, God asks us, *"Do you really think I've blessed you with so much just so you can goof off and take it easy? Do you really believe you're working only for yourself? That all this overflowing abundance is just for you?"* When we prioritize material blessings and tangible wealth instead of our treasure in heaven, we miss out on the fullness of more.

The riches of this life mean nothing in the economy of God.

Checklist for Success

So what really defines the fullness of your life? How would you describe your idea of a full life to someone else? How similar—or different—is it from the life you're living now? I know you know the "right" answers, but be honest with yourself—and remember that God already knows. I try to ask myself these questions regularly, especially when I'm tempted to shift back to a more human perspective on success.

Despite how much we may want to focus on spiritual things of eternal value, many of us struggle with letting go of that checklist in the back of our minds, this bucket list we carry for considering ourselves content and our lives worthwhile. Many times we created these checklists when we were young and just starting out and didn't have much. So we add a new BMW or Escalade or Ford F150 or whatever our dream car is to our list. Maybe you grew up like I did, moving around a lot, and at some point added a nice, big house in a beautiful, safe neighborhood to your list. Living paycheck to paycheck and struggling to pay your bills on time, you might have saving a certain dollar amount on your list.

The longer we live, we see what everyone else has and where they're going and how they're living—which is easier than ever thanks to social media—and we want the same things. A college degree. A loving spouse and healthy family. A fulfilling, well-paying career. Trips and vacations to exotic places. On and on our "success checklist" grows—new dreams, new goals, new hopes.

Please understand that wanting any of these things in and of itself isn't bad or sinful or displeasing to God—it's why you want them and what you want to do with them. The trap we so easily fall into is this: we define ourselves as successful only when we have most of if not all of our items checked off. Then our lives are full. Then we're experiencing the abundant life of blessings and enjoying God's more.

But that's not true!

The fullness of a life of more doesn't depend on anything except relying on God and serving his kingdom. Our lives are successful not if we own certain possessions, achieve particular milestones, or accomplish amazing feats. Our lives are successful if we live for God's glory every single day, growing closer to him, loving other people because of the way he first loved us, and sharing the blessings he has given us with those in need.

For the man who asked Jesus about his inheritance, fullness was in the hands of his brother and based on how their inheritance was divided. This guy basically felt like life was unfair because he wasn't getting what he felt he deserved, what he felt entitled to receive. He thought his life would be full and complete if his selfish brother would simply do the right thing and hand over some of what their mom and dad had left them. Because his brother refused, this guy then wanted Jesus to do something about it and make things right.

You and I are not so different. We get angry and frustrated and often ask God to intervene because we have to drive a car that's five years old, because we rent an apartment instead of owning a home, because we're paying off student loans that prevent us from accumulating wealth. We're looking for a newer car, a home we own, and a fatter bank account to make us full and complete. But once we have those items, we discover they aren't enough—we still want more.

The more we want will never be satisfied by anyone or anything on earth in this life. I don't care how complete another person looks. I don't care how successful they are. I don't care how much they own. No matter how much they have, it doesn't mean they're complete. They still have limitations.

According to God's Word, his ability to give to us, to bless, and to fulfill us is limitless! It has no ceiling, no roof, and no boundary. We're told, "Out of his fullness we have all received grace in place of grace already given" (John 1:16). When you or

I give something to someone, when we give them a blessing, we are left with less. If I give you some money so you can feed your family, I'm left with less, which means I need to go and work to make some more. If you're freezing cold during a harsh winter and I give you the coat off my back, then I have to buy another one. What one person can give to another person is limited by living in a physical world—no matter how much we want to give, our barrel is always going to have a bottom.

When God gives us a blessing, however, he can keep on giving. God does not need to work for more to supply your needs because God is complete and fulfilled all by himself. And when he gives you something, not only does he give you that particular gift or blessing, but he also gives you relationship, connection, and intimacy. He dwells in you and promises never to abandon you. He is all in.

God is himself the source of the fullness you long to experience deep in your bones, the contentment of having all you need, and the significance of giving all you have. He is a God who keeps on giving and never ends. He is a God who never finishes. He is so much more than money and possessions. When God gives, he gives of himself. His blessing is not limited to what you get, but who you get it with.

God is with you for the long haul.

Best If Used By

So many of the things we enjoy in this life last only for a short time. I know it sounds silly, but when I'm rummaging in the cabinet for a late-night snack, there's nothing worse than discovering the Cap'n Crunch cereal box is empty! Who leaves an empty box of cereal in the pantry? And what about that bag of Doritos with a "best if used by" date from last year!

Even if they're not labeled with an expiration date like most food items, most things never last as long as we'd like—clothes, cars, holidays, parties, vacations, just to name a few. In fact, most of the big variables we depend on to keep us going—people, jobs, resources, possessions—don't last that long either.

And what happens when the things that keep us going no longer work? Our kids grow up and move away, our parents grow old and pass away, coworkers come and go, and friends no longer have time for us. Companies close or downsize, homes get destroyed, cars need repair, trophies tarnish. No matter what sustains us in this world, it won't last—not forever and not when we need it most.

Only God endures, provides, and sustains you fully and completely in this life. This is why knowing him, loving him, and serving him should be at the center of your personal bull's-eye. If the storms take away your possessions, your relationships, and your status, God will still be there. And he can replenish every single thing that you have lost. God can replenish and redeem even the most painful, devastating losses if you will trust him to be all you need.

When what you get expires, it doesn't matter, because God is still with you. Everything you own will expire. Everything. Even your mortal body will expire. Everything you buy, everything you work for, everything you save, everything you store in your garage, your basement, and your attic will expire. None of it will last. It might be new today, but it will be old tomorrow. It's no wonder that God called the rich man in Jesus's parable a fool for tearing down his barns to build bigger ones and store more stuff.

There's only one thing without an expiration date in this life—your soul. Money and possessions, homes and cars, diamonds and dishrags will all come and go. Many of us worry so much about our investments and retirement funds, our 401(k)s and our stock portfolios, but as volatile economic times have shown us, no matter how hard we've worked and saved, our assets still go up and down.

God wants us investing in treasure that never depreciates, never spoils, never gets lost. Jesus told us, "Do not store up for yourselves treasures on earth, where moths and vermin destroy, and where thieves break in and steal. But store up for yourselves treasures in heaven, where moths and vermin do not destroy, and where thieves do not break in and steal. For where your treasure is, there your heart will be also" (Matt. 6:19–21).

If we're not attuned to what's going on in our hearts, and if our hearts aren't aligned with the Holy Spirit, then we lose sight of what's permanent and priceless. We end up focusing on temporary treasures and material matters on the surface of life instead of the eternal equity we could be building. We lose focus on our relationship with God and neglect talking to him and reading his Word.

And then we wonder why we still crave more!

Savor His Favor

Our souls, and the process of our spiritual growth, often get neglected because we become so busy, so distracted, so divided. We become tired, yet we keep going until we burn out. We attend to our aching bodies but overlook the hunger of our souls. While you and I need food, water, oxygen, and other elements to survive here on earth, God needs absolutely nothing. He is complete and whole and lacking in nothing. He satisfies us beyond anything we can eat, drink, breathe, purchase, rent, or consume in this life.

God gives us fullness of life because he alone can give us purpose. Your life has purpose because God has given it to you. Without purpose, you and I would go crazy. Without purpose, we wouldn't know what to do when we wake up in the morning. We wouldn't know why we're doing what we're doing or who we're working so hard for. The reason we get out of bed in the morning is because we have purpose. People who are depressed, who lose hope and resign themselves to an empty existence, have lost their purpose.

> *Without purpose, we wouldn't know what to do when we wake up in the morning.*

Our relationship with God colors our life as vividly as any masterpiece in the Art Institute of Chicago. We have someone to go to. We have somewhere to go. We have things that we have to do. God doesn't need anything because he has everything and can do anything. God is not dependent on what we do or don't do. He does not need us to worship him because he knows he is Lord with or without our praise. He does not need food to give him strength because he is the source of all power. He does not need counsel from anyone because he is the source of all wisdom. He does not need prayers in turmoil because he is the source of all peace.

And the amazing, illogical, crazy-hard thing to accept is that this almighty God shows his favor to you and me. He loves to bless us and give us good gifts as his sons and daughters.

We don't deserve it and can't earn it—God just loves us so much that he enjoys giving to us. He gives us grace and mercy, forgiveness and fresh starts. Even when we don't ask him, God still provides what we need. And just as important, he doesn't always give us what we ask for, protecting us from ourselves and our own selfish desires.

God's grace is not for the deserving. Grace is not some kind of point system, like the more good that I do, then eventually I'm going earn his favor. It doesn't work like that. God is full. And he shares his fullness, his completeness, his wholeness with people like you and me who are in desperate need. He gives us a blessed harvest beyond what we could have planted and nurtured on our own. None of us deserves to be in God's presence or to enjoy his favor. None of us deserved to have him send his only Son to die on a cross for us. None of us deserves eternal life in heaven with him.

All these things are pure gift-wrapped grace.

Full or Fool

Getting blessed with God's hand supersedes anything human hands can offer. People fall short and run out of what they can give you. God not only gives you enough, but he will always give you more than enough. People can bless you with moments of happiness, but only God blesses you with contentment. He even blesses you with joy in the midst of your sorrows and peace in the midst of life's storms.

When you think of all that you lack and fail to accomplish, God says, "I can provide what you need. Let me help you get back on your feet. Just take my hand." When you feel weak and powerless, unable to go another step, your Lord tells you, "My strength is sufficient in your weakness. You can do all things through Christ who strengthens you." Even when you face the toughest temptations imaginable, God gives you the power to resist their appeal and to defeat the devil.

God wants to keep you from being deceived. He reminds you of his truth in the midst of the appealing lies of the Enemy. God wants to protect you from a counterfeit life and from the emptiness that comes from chasing the world and all it offers. He wants you to learn and grow from your mistakes so that you may gain wisdom. If you'll obey him and allow him to guide you, God will protect you from yourself and the tendency to trust the desires of your heart more than him and his Word.

Haven't there already been times in your life when you have experienced God's protection and divine direction? And during those times, what kept you fooled for so long? What deceived you even as you knew what you were doing was not right in God's eyes? How many times have you believed your own lies and justifications rather than sought forgiveness and reconciliation?

Have you ever looked back on your life and thought, *Wow, I have no idea why I remained in that relationship for so long, why I kept going back to that addiction, why I let my pride come before others. I just couldn't get out of it.* We work so hard to experience the fullness of an abundant life. And time after time, we tend to base it on two things: our feelings and our circumstances. I believe we focus way too much on our feelings. I tell my church members you can't wait for a feeling before making a decision— you just have to know. If we waited for a feeling to prompt us to show up at church, most of us would never make it! But when we know that God is good and keeps his promises, we don't have to consider how we feel; we can just get up and go to church.

There's a passage in Scripture that I find helpful to better understand this way of "knowing": "This is the confidence we have in approaching God: that if we ask anything according to his will, he hears us. And if we *know* that he hears us— whatever we ask—we *know* that we have what we ask of him" (1 John 5:14–15, emphasis added).

When you live in the fullness of God, however, you shift your focus away from these two preoccupations of feelings and circumstances. Instead, you direct your time, attention, and energies toward knowing and serving him. You still wrestle with unpleasant emotions at times, but when you remind yourself of what is true and eternal, what God has done for you and how much he loves you, you can't help but feel better. You still get frustrated when circumstances don't go your way, but you can trust God to use them and change them even when that seems impossible or unimaginable.

When your soul is being replenished and filled with God's presence, you know God hasn't blessed you just so you can keep his blessings to yourself. He hasn't increased your harvest so you can build bigger barns and eat, drink, and be merry. You and I have been blessed by his grace, and God wants us to give away these same blessings to others. Jesus tells us to pray, "Forgive us our debts, as we also have forgiven our debtors" (Matt. 6:12), reminding us of the direct correlation between accepting God's forgiveness and forgiving others. If we truly know how much we have sinned against God and have been forgiven, then we have no claim against anyone who offends us.

When you become a Christian, you give up your right to

be offended. I believe one of the greatest deterrents to spiritual growth is offense. The way I keep myself from being offended is to remember Jesus on the cross. There, with his body nailed to two beams of wood, Jesus didn't say, "How could they do this to me? After everything I've done for them." Instead, the first thing out of his mouth was, "Father, forgive them." He refused to be offended. So I refuse to be offended.

When you become a Christian, you give up your right to be offended.

The more grace we've been given, the more grace we have to give away. If our response to the floodgates of heaven opening is to build bigger dams so that we can keep all the blessings for ourselves, then just like the man in Jesus's parable, we are fools. We are empty-headed as well as empty-hearted. When we focus only on ourselves and clutch what God has given us too tightly, I imagine him thinking, *Why would I give you more so that you can store it for next year? What good do you think it will do to sit on these blessings instead of sharing them with others? How can I keep blessing you with more if you're clinging to what I already gave you?*

Why be a fool when you can be full?

One More Blessing

No matter how much you succeed here on earth, how much you gain of this world, how much you accomplish, it will never satisfy your soul. It might satisfy your flesh, your body, your emotions, your ego for a little while. But it won't last, and your soul will still be crying out, starving for the Bread of Life.

Your soul is hungry. And your soul will never be satisfied with a new car, with a house at the beach, or with a billion dollars in the bank. But if you let go of chasing after those items for yourself, you will discover how good it feels to give away what you have to those who have nothing. It's the feeling many of us get at Christmas—we'd rather give than receive; we love surprising someone and seeing their face light up out of joy and gratitude. Their joy makes us light up! Being Christ's hands and feet, being his body and serving others—now that's food for the soul.

When you honor God with your obedience, you discover more and more of the fullness that comes only from knowing him. If you're going to have fullness of living in the more, it comes only from the riches of God. No more tears, no more worries, no more sickness, no more burdens, no more bills—hallelujah! Only peace and joy, pure comfort, and perfect contentment.

And we get a taste of it right now here on earth because of the relationship we have with the living God. He tells us, *"I know what you've been searching for and longing to experience. I have what your soul desires. I can give you what heaven offers. The fullness you're looking for—it's yours!"*

But you're not going to find it in this world. You're not going to find it in a relationship—not even in marriage. You're not going to find it in a bottle or a pill. You're not going to find it in an elite country club or on social media. You're not even going to find it in church—it's all about having a genuinely intimate relationship with God.

If you have God, you have everything you need.

Everything in your life is a blessing from God. Your home is a blessing. Your family is a blessing. Your church family is a blessing. The vehicle you drive, the place where you work, the food you ate today—all of it, blessing after blessing from a generous, loving God. He gives you an abundance so that you too can experience the joy of blessing others. The fullness of God is about receiving the blessings he has in store for you as you live out the purpose he has given you, which in turn blesses other people.

If you have God, you have everything you need.

And as our time together in these pages comes to an end, I pray God will use my humble efforts to bless you and change your understanding of what his more is all about. I encourage you to trust Jesus with the deepest longings of your heart, that hunger within for a more meaningful life, and see what he will do. Because no matter where you may be on your journey of faith, I know three things without a doubt.

God is there with you.

He wants to give you more.

And there's no limit to what he can do!

PRAYING FOR MORE

Lord, I have so many thoughts running through my mind as I think about what it means to live in your more. Thank you for speaking to my heart through these pages and challenging me to discover all that you have for me. I have been given so much, God, so please use me and all that I have to further your kingdom so that others may know you. I praise you for all that you're doing in my life and for all the more that's waiting ahead. Give me strength and courage to keep risking and trusting by the power of your Spirit, to keep stepping out in faith and growing closer to you each day. May I bless others as I have been blessed, in the fullness of discovering more of your love. Amen.

ENDNOTES

1. Kyle Chayka, "The Oppressive Gospel of Minimalism," *New York Times Magazine*, July 26, 2016, http://www.ny times.com/2016/07/31/magazine/the-oppressive-gospel -of-minimalism.html.
2. Beverly D. Flaxington, "The Epidemic of Insecurity," *Psychology Today*, April 7, 2015, https://www.psychology today.com/blog/understand-other-people/201504/the -epidemic-insecurity.

A life of faith isn't easy.
But it's worth it.

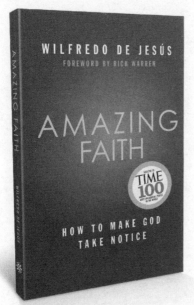

Be reminded by Wilfredo De Jesús that when you put yourself in God's hands without reservation—when you practice Amazing Faith—he will make you complete with his strength, love, and purpose.

Ebook also available.

AVAILABLE WHEREVER CHRISTIAN BOOKS ARE SOLD

978-1-93669-995-7 (English book)
978-1-93783-058-8 (Spanish book)

What happens when God's people stand strong

Wilfredo De Jesús explores nine biblical examples of God's people standing up for the vulnerable. Discover how making a difference for God will bring his grace and greatness into your life and the lives of others like never before.

Ebook also available.

Small group kit includes DVD and study guide. Components also sold separately.

AVAILABLE WHEREVER CHRISTIAN BOOKS ARE SOLD

978-1-93830-989-2 (English book)
978-1-62912-114-7 (English small group kit)

978-1-93830-992-2 (Spanish book)
978-1-62912-115-4 (Spanish small group kit)

If you feel like the culture is shifting under your feet and you're powerless to get it back on track, you're not alone. Many of us see the powerful undercurrents of history that are taking place before our eyes. In response, some people sink into hopelessness, while others struggle desperately to remain strong in their faith.

Pastor Choco De Jesús offers real hope and practical solutions. He clearly identifies the pressures of the culture, acknowledges our human tendency to drift, and provides biblical encouragement to "stay the course" in our walks with God. Combining powerful stories with surprising insights and sound biblical principles, Pastor Choco helps us discover God's path and follow it through good times and bad, always drawing closer to him.

AVAILABLE WHEREVER CHRISTIAN BOOKS ARE SOLD

978-0-9973372-2-8 (print)
978-0-9973372-3-5 (ebook)